TABLE OF CONTENTS

INTRODUCTION

To understand others is to be knowledgeable;
To understand yourself is to be wise.

To conquer others is to have strength;
To conquer yourself is to be strong.

—*Tao Te Ching*

Before introducing this wild tale of synchronicity, I feel it is important to examine the idea of faith, to give the reader clarity as to what I mean when I am talking about faith. *The Depth of Synchronicity* is essentially about a strange process of self-discovery that has required a great deal of faith. Not the faith that one has in what they are told to believe, but rather the type of faith that comes from direct experience. The fruits of that experience having been so sweet, as to inspire faith in an outlandish path, even if the trail-blazing seems to contradict widely accepted models of reality.

The great scholar Erich Fromm categorizes the idea of faith into two contrasting existential modes: Having and Being. The *having mode* of existence is characterized by ownership, control, and necrophilia, while the *being mode* involves appreciation, free-thinking, and encouraging the natural process of growth. Fromm begins by describing faith in the *having mode* of existence:

Faith, in the having mode, is the possession of an answer for which one has no rational proof. It consists of formulations created by others, which one accepts because one submits to those others-- usually a bureaucracy. It is the entry ticket to join a large group of people. It relieves one of the hard tasks of thinking for oneself and making decisions...
Faith, in the having mode, gives certainty; it claims to pronounce ultimate, unshakable knowledge, which is believable because the power of those who promulgate and protect the faith seem unshakable.

It isn't uncommon to see this type of faith in religion, politics, education, science, business, social groups, family, medicine, culture, media, etc. Society seems to be immersed in narratives that are taken at face value, without questioning, investigating, or critically examining the many factors, variables, or unknown and yet to be discovered pieces of a puzzle. This type of submissive faith has proven to be dangerous; causing violence, poverty, prejudice, war, genocide, and all manner of maligned group behavior.

Fromm contrasts the having mode of faith, with a type of faith propagated by those who live in what he calls the *being mode* of existence:

My faith in myself, in another, in humankind, in our capacity to become fully human also implies certainty, but certainty based on my own experience and not on my submission to an authority that dictates a certain belief. It is certainty of a truth that cannot be proven by rationally compelling evidence, yet truth I am certain of because of my experiential, subjective evidence.

The story of Jesus (Yeshua) or Buddha, may serve as examples of a life lived in the being mode of faith. Both believed in the virtue of their spiritual path, while the health and healing of their works demonstrated evidence for the power of their subjective experience. They taught people to love one another, and even to "love your enemies" and "do good to them that hate you."

However, in examining the history of the Catholic church and those who follow the church with the having mode of faith, we see some of the greatest violence, war, and genocide in history. What was supposedly built around the life and teachings of Jesus Christ, seems to have been hijacked by the having mode of faith, and ironically violence and fear forced or coerced many into joining the Catholic institution.

On the contrary to violent religious dogma, if one in the being mode of faith shares their subjective experience with others who are inspired to question, test, critique, and consider the possibility of the information as something potentially helpful, or not helpful, then the being mode of faith can be transferred in a positive way, inspiring others to have their own healthy unique subjective experience that isn't limited or controlled by group dogma.

We have historical examples of Christian mystics who were inspired by the teachings of Christ, but not limited by the dogma of the church. In this way they had a greater ability to realize and live Christ's teaching to love your neighbor and your enemies. One such example of a Christian mystic is cited in the writings of Erich Fromm and Carl Jung. He was a medieval friar referred to as Master Eckart.

According to Fromm, Eckart exemplifies the being mode of existence within the confines of a dogmatic institution. As Jesus said, **"The Kingdom of God is within you,"** and Eckart echoed this idea in his teachings and sermons. The idea that god is present in each soul sounds like an eastern philosophy, or an indigenous belief, and yet Christ clearly communicates this idea, as did Master Eckart. As a result, Eckart became so popular in the 13th century, that he was tried for heresy by the catholic church. His being mode of faith was threatening the institutional having mode of faith.

I find it pertinent to share Fromm's ideas about faith in this introduction, because I am about to share a story that I cannot prove with "rationally compelling evidence". And yet this adventure tale has required a great deal of faith on my part. I ask the reader not to believe my story with the having mode of faith, as it is not a dogmatic approach to spirituality. However, I rather hope to inspire the reader to explore the being mode of faith, following one's experience of synchronicity.

I developed my being mode of faith by following a bread crumb trail, spanning from one subjective experiential piece of evidence to another. The breadcrumb analogy of subjective evidence began as little pieces along the trail, but often led to a very tasty loaf, or in some cases quite a magical bakery.

I began with a great deal of naivety and a brain full of standard public-school American education and mass media programming. Like many Americans I was deeply entrenched in the having mode of nationalistic faith. However, in going to college I began a process of unlearning information that was based on authoritative hierarchy, and for the first time in my life I learned to do my own research and think critically. However, this process was just the beginning of opening me up to a more subjective experiential mode of learning and being.

O N E

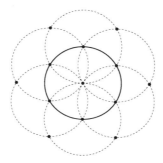

THE POTENT PART of my story begins during a meditation. I was on the porch of a remote rustic cabin in Waipio Valley on the Big Island of Hawaii. I was born and raised in Hawaii, and I have lived there all my life. In the valley I was surrounded by exotic fruit trees, streams of water, and wetland taro patches. The time-period was in the first week of January 2005, and I would be 23 years old in April of that year.

During my meditation there were hundreds of birds sounding off in unison around sunset, and I began to feel like I was communicating with them in my mind. It felt like my internal dialogue was having a conversation with the external environment. I could hear the rhythm of the birds and the wind blowing in the trees, synchronized to thoughts I was observing in my meditation.

As I was meditating on inner-outer communication, I began to hear neighboring animals such as dogs, crickets, roosters, horses, and pigs, all sounding off in a sort of symphony, that seemingly began all at once like a response to my meditative thoughts. It felt like a validation from the animals in the valley, like they were responding to my thoughts about communication. Subsequently, I had the thought that if everything outside of me is a sort of communication from spirit, or type of reflective symbolism, then every physical sensation I experience in my body is also a communication from spirit. Every good feeling and sensation, and every itch or pain, translating like a message from my soul to my body and mind.

Having this revelation, suddenly my meditation deepened, my thoughts seemed to vanish, and I was entranced by the sounds around me. An energy like an electric sensation moved quickly through me from the bottom of my spine to the top of my head. My spine cracked into place like a chiropractic adjustment, my ears popped, and my sinus cleared all at once. I felt surprised, amazed, perfect, top shape, better than I ever had before. It was as if time stopped for a moment, my body became light, and all fear, worry and doubt transformed into love and excitement.

What came next was so subtle, yet so profound and life changing, I don't exactly have the words to describe what it means to me. **I noticed a subtle tingling sensation on the top left side of my forehead**. Because of my previous meditative thoughts, I assumed this was a subtle form of communication from spirit. I slowly turned my head in that direction looking to the left. Just as I looked left, a motion sensor porch light turned on and shown onto the wetland Taro patch next to the house. The porch light felt like a synchronous validation. I stood up and walked in that direction until I was standing ankle deep in the water of the Taro Patch where the light was shining. I then began to feel more tingling sensations moving around on various parts of my body intermittently as if they were directing me to slowly move my fingers, hands, arms, feet, legs, back, neck, and head. I moved my body with the direction of the sensations in slow thai chi or chi gong type movements (however, up to that point in my life I had been unfamiliar with chi movement practices).

For the next week I diligently followed these tingling sensations around the valley experiencing a constant state of meditative synchronicity. At times I moved extremely slowly. For example, when I felt the tingling sensation on my back, I interpreted it as suggesting that I slow down, and I would walk with very slow deliberate meditative movements, or wash dishes extremely slowly. I would often completely stop walking and perform various chi-like movements, depending on what I felt my tingling sensations were guiding me to do. It was a constant communicative adventure of figuring out what these sensations meant depending on where they manifested on my body. My body became like a map written in an obscure language, or an ancient navigational instrument, and it was my task to decipher or perhaps develop what each tingling location meant.

These systems I developed through meditation, trial and error. I began to notice that feelings in my eyes had significant meaning. Sometimes my eyes felt itchy or dry and irritated, other times they felt moist and relaxed. Often one eye felt different than the other. I interpreted each eye to represent a major portion of myself, in that my left eye responds to my actions or creativity, while my right eye is responding to thinking and reasoning. In this way I was able to filter my inner and outer reality interpretations and actions. To this day when I am in a deep mediation or subconscious healing process, my eyes become very moist and relaxed.

The other system I developed or interpreted involved the tingling sensations I would feel on my face. A tingling on my chin would tell me to stop doing or to avoid something. Tingling on my forehead was an indication to go or move toward something I was thinking about doing. The tip of my nose or upper lip involved feeling like I was on the right path, a validation to keep going. Tingling on my ear would encourage me to listen carefully, often bringing me important synchronous auditory information. I will elaborate more on these systems later, as this information is just to give the reader an idea of my interpretation of these subtleties.

These interpretations evolved and developed over time, depending on the context and subjective content of the moment. What I am uncertain of is how much of this process has been intuitive interpretation versus how much I developed or created these ideas as a sort of agreement between me and my higher mind. What I do know is that these systems work with profound accuracy. In the next chapter I will share profound stories that led me to the validation of this depth of synchronicity.

However, I was skeptical and questioned my practice and the nature of this tingling sensation. It felt very real, and the effects from it were well appreciated, however my habitual American made mind wondered if I was going crazy. I had never heard of anyone following around tingling sensations that they feel on their skin. If I wasn't going crazy, then what was I doing? Was I tapping into an energy field or spirit that was exclusive to the valley, or was this something that was more universal? Perhaps the subtle spirit energy described in the Tao? Was I the only person who had experienced this, or was there someone with a similar experience? I had many questions and not one person I could consult on the matter.

The experience I had with these two women gave me a profound sense of validation. I realized that events could be manifested in the most magical ways, and that my perception of this tingling sensation could **predetermine synchronous moments with profound accuracy**. I had just met both women for the first time in that same day, in a city with nearly one million people in it, and I was able to link the two of them together in perfect timing, and in a way that helped a lost girl get to her friend's house safely.

What still boggles my mind about this event, is the predetermination of the tingling sensations on my skin to guide me to these two women and manifest the timing in such a way that I could clearly see that this **phenomenal sensitivity had a sort of intelligence** that seemed to predict the future. By placing me with the first girl to get a sense of her location and who she was, so that I would later recognize a description of her, to the point that I would be able to guide her lost friend to her house, the event was orchestrated with brilliant time and space precision that left zero possibility for mere chance or random coincidence. In other words, this was very obviously divinely orchestrated by a higher mind **beyond my own egoic personality structure**.

This was one of many similarl validating experiences. These experiences were a boost to continue down the path, adding greater confidence to my perceptions.

A few months prior, during the summer of 2005, I was living in Chico, CA renting a room from a friend. I was in my room one evening listening to the local college radio station. The DJ was interviewing two young men who were making a sort of poetic type of hip hop that was very enjoyable to listen to. In the interview one of the young men, the music producer Jacob (also known as

DJ Story), mentioned that he would be going to Kauai. I instantly thought about my friend Tiana on Kauai who has beautiful singing voice and loves conscious hip hop. I imagined that it would be cool to link them up on the island when he got there. The feeling was so strong I almost called the radio station to contact Jacob about Tiana. However, I rather chose to let it go and forgot about it.

A few days later I got up in the morning and followed my tingling synchronicity out of the house and walked into town. There was a music festival going on and I followed my spider senses to a very specific place in the crowd facing the stage. During my travels I would often walk around following the direction of tingles on my face until I felt it tingling on my chin. I interpreted a tingling on my chin to mean stop. As soon as I felt the tingle on my chin at the festival I stopped and faced the stage watching the music performance.

When the performance finished I heard a recognizable voice speaking to someone behind me. At first, I couldn't place the voice, and then after a few minutes of hearing him talk it struck me who it was. I turned around and said, "Hey were you on the radio a few nights ago?"

"Yea you heard that?!" he said with a look of surprise.

"Are you the one going to Kauai soon?"

"No that's my friend Jacob, DJ Story who produces the beats. I'm the vocalist poet. But he's here too, I can introduce you to him."

As I'm writing this I can't remember the poet vocalist's name, so I inserted "vocalist poet" where his name would be. Please bear with me on that aspect, as I am not a professional ethnographer with proper notes from 13 years ago. However, he did take me to meet DJ Story/Jacob whose name I do remember.

After Jacob/DJ Story and I were introduced, he invited me to his parents' house for dinner, along with his vocalist poet buddy. Jacob's mother was cooking a wonderful natural foods dinner, while Jacob took me on a tour of their house. It was a beautiful place with gardens and a little stream running through it. He showed me his music studio where they recorded and made songs. Jacob had a peaceful, creative, soft spoken personality. He seemed open minded and excited, as if he was taking in the adventure of life and finding his place in it.

I explained to all of them about the fantastic synchronicity of hearing DJ Story/Jacob on the radio, and associating his trip to to Kauai with my friend Tiana who lives there, only to meet him a few days later by hearing his friend's voice behind me at the music festival. Jacob was especially impressed with my synchronicity story. He even invited another friend over that he thought would want to hear my story, perhaps living up to his stage name DJ Story. I felt comfortable sharing more deeply about the mechanism of following my tingling spider sense. They were spiritually minded people, and they responded to my story with excitement. I remember his friend telling me that he thought more and more people would be doing something like what I was doing with my spider sense. He believed that the awareness of synchronicity would be more conscious as humanity evolved into a more spiritually minded culture.

After leaving Jacob's house, I contacted Tiana on Kauai, and I told her the story. I explained that I intended to connect her with Jacob for music making opportunities and good vibes. She was excited about the idea and asked me to give Jacob her number. She enjoyed hearing about the synchronicity and that I had associated her with him.

After that I went about my life, following my spider senses as usual, enjoying little adventures. Then a few weeks had gone by when I got a call from Tiana. She was excited to share some news with me. She began by telling me that DJ Story hadn't called her at all before he left for Kauai. Apparently, when DJ Story/Jacob landed on Kauai his friend picked him up from the airport in Lihue. I will refer to Jacob's friend as the airport-guy for the convenience of telling this story. Airport-guy drove Jacob directly from the airport to the health food store called Papaya's in Kapa'a (about a fifteen-minute drive). When Jacob and his friend got to Papaya's they randomly ran into one of airport-guy's friends, who was a dark-skinned long-haired picturesque local Hawaiian girl. Airport-guy explained to her that he had just picked up Jacob from the airport, and the local girl said to Jacob, "Aloha, I'm Tiana, welcome to Kauai!" and she kissed him on the cheek, which is a customary Hawaiian welcome greeting. Jacob looked at her with shock and surprise and said, "Tiana... are you Ben's friend?!"

Tiana then explained to me that they all marveled at the synchronicity of the story. From the moment I heard Jacob on the radio, I associated him with Tiana when he mentioned going to Kauai during his radio interview. What are the chances that Jacob would meet Tiana as soon as he arrived on Kauai? She was literally the first person that he randomly met after getting off the plane, and she was friends with the guy who picked him up from the airport.

Hearing Tiana tell me this story greatly increased my validation of synchronicity as meaningful coincidences or divinely orchestrated events. Seeing how the synchronicity impacted Tiana and Jacob inspired me to realize that what I was doing could **facilitate others to have magical experiences** that benefited their lives. There was no way for me to know the extent of how much I was benefitting or inspiring people, I only knew that I could feel their excitement and interest spark. And yet in some scenarios I would be completely baffled at what synchronicity did for a person, and all I could perceive was that they were deeply emotionally effected. My next story describes such an event.

When I got back to the Big Island, I worked and lived at my friend's coffee farm in Kaloko. I would often eat lunch at a nearby place called Kay's Kitchen. One day as I was having lunch, a middle-aged woman sat down at the table across from me. She was well dressed, normal and average looking, but writing in a little notebook that looked like a personal journal.

After a few minutes I began to have the strong feeling that I could write a sort of spiritual health and healing equation for this woman in her notebook. This was an equation that I had written previously in my own journal, so I was familiar with how to write it. But this was the first time I had ever thought to write it for another person.

I didn't hesitate, and I asked her point blank, "Can I write you something in your notebook?"

She looked at me skeptically, and I don't blame her. We had never met before, I didn't introduce myself or open the conversation up with something light and normal. I suppose its not every day that a random person asks to write in your personal journal. However, after a moment she agreed and handed me her notebook. I wrote the following:

$$Peace = Contentment = Ease$$

$$Desire = Discontentment = Dis\text{-}Ease$$

Therefore, Desire and Disease are closely related.

*Those who are constantly without desire, perceive
the subtlety of the way of heaven.*

I gave the woman her notebook and I went back to eating my lunch. I became focused on enjoying my plate of food, and so it was a surprise to me when 5 or so minutes later the woman sat down at my table with tears rolling down her cheeks.

Speaking through her tears she asked me, "Do you know why you wrote this?" I answered honestly and shook my head no, because I didn't know why I wrote it.

She then asked me, "Do you know who this is from?" I nodded yes, because it was my interpretation that I was channeling spirit. After I nodded yes, she burst into tears and said through a whisper, "Thank you," and then she got up and left.

To this day I don't know specifically what I did for that woman, other than a profound release of emotions, and perhaps a shift in her beliefs. I realize now that when I nodded yes, my interpretation of who that equation came from, may have been different than her interpretation. I'm not sure who exactly she had in mind, but in my mind this message came from my higher mind, the same mind that communicates with me through tingling sensations, symbols and signs, synchronicity, visions, etc.

I want to be clear that when I say, "my higher mind", I believe that everyone has a higher mind that orchestrates these types of synchronicity experiences for them, even if they aren't aware of it. I believe that these types of experiences are often designed to grab a person's attention and wake them up to something they may need to pay more attention to. My own awareness of synchronicity began with experiences that woke me up to the spiritual magic that is infused into everyday life. Although I didn't fully understand it and could barely grasp the who, what, how, and why of it, I would eventually find answers the more I allowed the path to unfold, which has led me to the belief in a higher mind.

Although the experiences I describe in this chapter, along with many others, gave me increased trust and faith in the concept of synchronicity, and the depth to which I was experiencing it, at that time I still did not have the spiritual knowledge or scientific context to explain what was happening and how it was happening. All I knew at the time was that I had the will to follow this path, regardless of how crazy or strange it seemed to family and friends, or even to myself. I remember being inspired by a quote from the movie Apocalypse Now, "Can you free yourself from the opinions of others, or even the opinions of yourself?"

Although I came into this spiritual path lacking contextual information, I had the open mind and humility to learn, combined with a sort of naïve but profound personal experience. My path was about to take me on a journey of discovery, in which I would learn about quantum physics, spiritual philosophy, emotional intelligence, communication, holistic health, herbalism, nutrition, detoxification, and a variety of meditation techniques. This information would provide me with a greater context to understand the tingling spider sense synchronicity that had become the foundation of my life path. I would also learn additional skill sets to build on that foundation, developing a holistic tool kit for health, healing, and living a joyful life.

PREQUEL

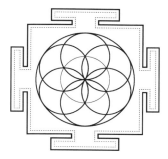

As a youth I was conflicted about spirituality. My Mom was slightly Christian, and my Dad was a non-practicing Jew. Neither of them expressed much spirituality, and they came from different familial religious backgrounds. My Mom would go to church on holidays like Easter and Christmas. With my Dad we would celebrate Christmas at home, even though he was raised Jewish. He thought of Christmas as more of a consumer holiday with the Santa Claus motif. Hanukah and Passover celebrations were the extent of our Jewish practice. So it was quite a journey for me to discover spirituality and define what that meant for me as an ever growing and evolving process.

My early memories of having spiritual ideas were the feeling that there was more to reality than what meets the eye, but I didn't know how to explain it or put it into words. I felt that I believed in God and Spirit, but that was about the extent of what I felt intuitively.

My Dad didn't hesitate to crush those beliefs when he told me at a young age, "There's no such thing as spirits or God."

After that, and for most of my childhood, I blocked out my connection to source. It wasn't until my high school senior English class that I opened myself to spiritual ideas. It was at that time that I had my first introduction to the Tao Te Ching, Buddhism, and general eastern philosophy. I owe a lot to that class, and yet this only laid a superficial foundation for what was to come. I learned about the ideas and philosophies as spiritual concepts, but I had no real experience to connect them with. It wasn't until my **first undeniable awareness of synchronicity** that I felt an experiential spiritual foundation.

I can vividly remember the first time I experienced the awareness of a synchronous event. I was in my first year of college at UH Hilo, the year was 2001 (It wasn't until 2005 that I would have my life changing Waipio valley tingling spider sense discovery). I was driving my car through town and listening to a song by *cLOUD-DEAD* titled *Bicycle Part 2*. The song has two vocalists, and one of the artists named *Why?* sings an acapella line, "Edison fix my glasses like new." As the word glasses came through the speakers of my car, I happened to look to my left and simultaneously saw the word glasses on a neon sign advertising eye glasses for a shop. I heard and saw the word glasses in the exact same timing and it floored me sending "chills" and "goosebumps" through my body.

The timing of seeing and hearing the word glasses could not have been more precisely simultaneous. 'What are the chances?' I asked myself.

How could these two seemingly unrelated items match up perfectly in a moment in which they have such a small window of time to come together. If I had started the song a few seconds later or listened to a different song, took a different route, left my house at a different time, or didn't look to the left at that moment, there would be no chance for the two "glasses" to sync up.

The other aspect was the emotional feeling that I had just experienced something profound. Before pondering or considering the phenomena, **I immediately felt a sense of connection to the universe.** It was like I woke up and realized in an instant that I am connected to something greater than myself.

I eventually realized that glasses are symbolic of perspective and perception, representing the way we look at things. That moment gave me a new pair of glasses. I became excited to explore and connect with spirit, seeing things in a new light. Thomas Edison, who is mentioned in the opening lyric, "Edison fix my glasses like new," was involved in developing the light bulb. A light bulb is often represented symbolically when someone has an epiphany, and this was one of the most memorable epiphany moments of my life.

However, I lacked spiritual context or metaphysical information at that time in my life, and none of these symbols were immediately relevant to me. Up to that point in time I had been exposed to Taoism and Buddhism in high school but only from an intellectual perspective, and there was so much of it that went over my head and missed my heart and soul, as I wasn't ready to receive it.

This memorable experience with synchronicity was an important time in my conscious life in which I felt connected to spirit, and yet I didn't know what that meant or how to contextualize it. I had a feeling, but I lacked the framework to define or ground it.

At that point in my life I hadn't heard the word or concept of synchronicity. I didn't know much about shamanism or symbolism.

I had never heard of quantum physics, metaphysics, or new age philosophy. To some degree I was spiritually lost, but I had just found a breadcrumb and my eyes were now open looking for more.

Over the next few years I immersed myself in the study of spirituality and philosophy, while practicing a spiritual awareness of increased synchronicity and connectivity. In the summer of 2003 when I was 21, I traveled to Paris for my cousin's college graduation, and I stayed with her in Paris for a few weeks. It was here that I experienced a much more profound synchronicity, involving similar themes.

About a week or so into my stay in Paris, I woke up one morning and put on an album by a group called *Themselves*. The vocalist for *Themselves*, *Dose* (also known as *Doseone*), was one of the two vocalists for the group *cLOUDDEAD*. *Dose* is featured in that same song *Bicycle 2* alongside the vocalist called *Why?* (*Why?* is the vocalist that says "Edison fix my glasses like new"). The point being that *Dose* of *Themselves* is connected to the first synchronicity I described in this chapter.

As I was in my cousin's small Parisian apartment enjoying my morning, drinking a cup of tea, and listening to *Themselves*, I decided to go on the internet to look up their touring schedule. I was hoping to maybe catch one of their shows in the U.S on my way back to Hawaii. It seemed like a longshot because I would only be in California (bay area) for a few days, but I hoped I might get lucky or rather synchronous. As I browsed the website, to my utter amazement I discovered that *Themselves* was playing a show in Paris that day!

I did a double take to make sure that I was seeing the tour schedule correctly. I was shocked that they were playing a show in

Paris on the exact day I was looking at their schedule. The other odd aspect was that I wasn't in the habit of looking up tour schedules online. Having lived most of my life on the Big Island, I wasn't used to music shows coming to the island. This was probably the first time it had ever even occurred to me to look up any musician's touring schedule.

I was in a state of excited surprise and amazement. However, when I called the music venue I was disappointed to find out that the show was already sold out. As quickly as the feelings of amazement had arisen, they were beginning to diminish. However, I quickly developed another exciting idea- that I should just go to the music venue right away. I got dressed and left the house on an adventure to find my way through the streets of Paris to this obscure art and music venue. **I remained in a confident state of mind that I could make it happen, and yet without stressing or expecting any particular outcome.**

When I arrived at the location, I was happily surprised to recognize *Dose* of *Themselves* unloading sound gear from the tour van. As soon as I saw him I knew my intuition and persistence was about to pay off. I walked right up to him and said, "Hey Dose". He looked at me smiling and said, "What's up man, my names Adam." I told him that I wanted to see his show, but that it was sold out. He told me it was no problem to put me on the guest list, and just like that I was in!

I helped them (*Themsleves*) unload the van. I watched them set up and practice. I got to hang out with some of the other poet/ vocalists that were there like *Sage Francis* and *Sole*. I went for a walk with *Sole* in which we obtained some cannabis for the crew and cruised around Paris. I was like a kid in a candy shop spending time with some of my favorite musicians on a synchronous adventure.

Themselves gave an epic performance that was much better than I expected. I enjoyed the sound of their live performance even more than their recorded album. It was the perfect ending to a surprisingly eventful day.

That synchronicity was huge for me. These independent hip hop artists were like my version of celebrities. I had followed their music for years and had previous synchronous experiences with *Dose's* music, as I mentioned earlier. Then suddenly and very unexpectedly I was hanging out with them in Paris of all places. The experience helped me grow into a more magical shamanistic synchronous mind state, that would mature my sense of spirituality, and encourage an openness to more profound synchronicity.

Life can be magical beyond what we imagine. Planning is all well and good, but if we stay open to what is possible, and don't put an expectation or confinement on the outcome, then it becomes possible for much greater things to happen beyond what we can imagine. I had planned to go to Paris to visit my cousin, but I left much of the trip open to chance/synchronicity. When I went on the internet that morning to look up *Themselves* tour schedule, I never could have imagined I would be hanging out with *Themselves* (plus Sole and Sage Francis) within the same day. Life was wide open for me in that moment, and therefore I was able to manifest beyond what I thought was possible.

About a year later in 2004 I began to experience a major identity conflict. My world was unraveling. I had been studying at UH Hilo on and off with no idea as to why or what I was doing there. I was in a relationship with a woman that I wasn't comfortable sharing my spiritual outlook with, and it felt like I was suppressing too much of myself. I would often go out hiking to find a place to meditate and connect with nature. I would sometimes eat mushrooms as a sort of permission slip to connect with more of myself, enjoying wonderful expansive experiences. However, when I came back from these trips I would try to suppress myself again when I became sober, regressing to the constraints of what I thought society expected of me. I was dividing myself to an unbearable point, and **I could no longer hold back the momentum of knowing who I am and why I am here.**

That fall semester we were reading Nietzsche's **Beyond Good and Evil**, Marx's **Communist Manifesto**, and other very interesting material in a class called Philosophy of Liberalism. This was combined with a constant study of the **Tao Te Ching** that sent me into a vortex of identity unraveling. I was noticeably snapping out of the matrix for better, and at times for worse. My friends who understood seemed entertained and wanted to be around me at that time. For my family and those who couldn't understand, it looked unstable. I was falling into a flow that would lead me to be myself, and to truly find myself, but I didn't know how to do it without making very striking choices, like not showing up for finals and just completely **dropping out of school** near the end of the semester.

During that time, I had obtained a copy of the Tao that was a Robert Henricks translation of the recently discovered **Ma-wang-tui texts**, the oldest version of the Tao that had been found. I became obsessed with contemplating desire, a theme often mentioned in Taoism, "The sage desires not to desire."

The first chapter of the Tao reads:

As for the Way, the Way that can be spoken of is not the constant Way;

As for names, the name that can be
named is not the constant name.

The nameless is the beginning of the ten thousand
things (the earth and all its features);

The named is the mother of the ten thousand things.

The next part of the first chapter is what fixated my attention during the fall of 2004, leading up to my time in Waipio valley and the discovery of my tingling sensations. I credit this next passage of the first chapter with being the most influential in my path:

Therefore those constantly without desires, by this
means will perceive its (the way of heaven) subtlety.

Those constantly with desires, by this means will
see only that which they yearn for and seek.

These two together emerge;

They have different names yet they're called the same;

That which is even more profound than the profound-

The gateway of all subtleties.

These verses gave me a spiritual goal. I could see that I had been driven by my own desires, which had caused me to see only that which I yearned for sought. In doing so I narrowed the scope of what I could manifest, and limited my consciousness blocking my ability to know and expand more deeply into learning about myself. I wanted to be *constantly without desires* and *perceive its subtlety*; even though I didn't really understand or know what *it* was. I was in a confused and polarizing state. In the Tao it says:

through a process of remembering and experiencing reality, growth, and transformation from new and unique perspectives.

I have spent more than 13 years experiencing both sides of this path (dark and light), and I have just now worked up the courage to write this story. I find it fascinating that I made this discovery in my youth with very little context or understanding. However, part of the adventure has been to find spiritualists, psychologists, physicists, and biologists that give a scientific, cultural, and historical basis for my experience of spiritual alchemy and the depth of synchronicity.

CONTEXT

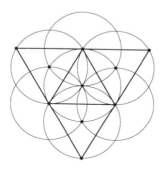

MANY OF THE WORLDS great thinkers and scientists were first struck by profound experiences that led them to research and develop new ways of thinking. C.G Jung, largely considered one of the greatest minds of our time, tells the story of his academic career in a similar way. Jung was inspired by phenomena that didn't fit into the narrow lens of consensus reality, causing him to develop the concept of synchronicity.

As a young man, Jung witnessed a solid oak table suddenly split and break apart. Within moments he saw a steel knife break into pieces. Both events happened apparently without a cause. His superstitious mother was there to witness the events, and she looked at him in such a way that made him think on the matter. He learned that other members of his family had been participating in seances, and they had wanted to invite him. This synchronous event stimulated him to join the seances, which led him down a path of interest in occult phenomena, that he would later develop in the academic arena coining the word *Synchronicity* to explain seemingly "acausal" events and **"meaningful coincidences"**.

Jung would eventually cross paths with Albert Einstein and physicist Professor W. Pauli. He explains that his relationship and conversations with these physicists helped him develop his thesis of psychic synchronicity. In one of Jung's letters, responding to Pauli he writes, "Synchronicity could be understood as an ordering system by means of which similar things coincide, without there being any apparent cause."

It seems that what modern physicists have learned about the nature of reality and sub-atomic particles may suggest that Jung's concept of synchronicity is not the exception to the rule, but perhaps the way in which reality operates. In this chapter I describe some of the theories of leading **quantum physicists** to explain the notion that came to me while meditating on the porch in Waipio valley as explained in chapter 1 of this book: 'I had the thought that if everything outside of me is a sort of communication from spirit, or type of reflective symbolism, then every physical sensation I experience in my body is also a communication from spirit. Every good feeling and likewise every pain or irritation translating like a message.'

University of London physicist David Bohm, like Jung, was struck by experiences that led him to rethink the nature of reality. For Bohm, as a physicist, that meant looking deeper into quantum theory. Bohm's personal experience began while working with plasma at the Lawrence Berkley Radiation Laboratory. What Bohm discovered was that while electrons (sub-atomic particles) were in a plasma, they were observed to work together like an organism. Vast numbers of electrons were able to produce organized efforts, such obscure ancient texts that were showing up in his patients dreams and hallucinations. This led Jung to believe that there was a collective unconscious in which archetypes common to humanity manifested as communications to the conscious mind through dreams and visions.

What Jung is calling the unconscious, is perhaps what shamans and ancient cultures refer to as spirit or god. It is perhaps what Bohm is calling quantum potential. And it is perhaps the source of intelligent communication I experience through tingling sensations on my skin, and the reality I experience as synchronicity.

What David Bohm described as a *holomovement*, is the idea that everything is an expression of one interconnected thing. The One Thing that we call God, Great Spirit, or All that Is, experiences itself through all of the unique perspectives and aspects of creation. It is essentially formless in the sense that it is found in every form.

The Emerald Tablet by Hermes Thoth, shares this perspective:

That which is Below corresponds to that which is Above,

and that which is Above corresponds to that which is Below,

to accomplish the miracles of the One Thing.

And just as all things have come from this One Thing,

through the meditation of One Mind,

through Transformation.

Similarly, from the **Tao Te Ching by Lao Tzu:**

The Way gave birth to the One;

The One gave birth to the Two;

The Two gave birth to the three;

And the Three gave birth to the Ten Thousand Things (the earth and all its features).

The Ten Thousand Things carry Yin on their backs and wrap their arms around Yang.

Through a blending of ch'i (energy) they arrive at a state of harmony.

-Translated by Robert G. Henricks, based on the Ma-wang-tui texts

The Emerald Tablet is an ancient text that is widely credited as the foundational text of western alchemy. Many books and stories about alchemy reference the Emerald Tablet and its ancient author Hermes Thoth. The Tao Te Ching, authored by Lao-Tzu, is the foundation for Chinese Alchemy and much of Chinese philosophy. The idea of the **One** is the foundational basis for both eastern and western alchemy; seemingly related to the conclusions drawn from quantum theory, and Jung's collective unconscious. As I sat on the porch of the cabin in Waipio, feeling as though my mind was communicating with the birds in the trees and everything surrounding me, I certainly felt the connectivity of Oneness, which led to the transformation of my entire life path through a great depth of synchronicity.

After I left Waipio Valley, and traveled to California, the first place I went to was Los Angeles. I was following my tingling sensations around as usual, with no idea of where I was going or what I was doing. I wandered into a Jewish neighborhood called Fairfax. I found my way to a theatre that was playing just one movie, it was called ***What the Bleep Do We Know?*** It was a documentary about quantum physics, biology, and spirituality. It combined scientific discovery with the spiritual notion that we are all connected to source, god, spirit and each other. This was my first introduction to the type of science that gave me a context for what I was experiencing with synchronicity.

One of the scientists interviewed was biologist and author Dr. Bruce Lipton. In his book, The Biology of Belief, Lipton explains how he came to discover that the behavior of cells is largely influenced by environment, nutrients, toxins, and beliefs. Stressful or negative beliefs send signals to cells that can create diseases and problems in our DNA. Relaxed or positive beliefs send health and healing signals to our cells. There are a variety of signals from a variety of beliefs. This mechanism in cell biology is called **signal transduction.**

When we combine the idea of belief generated signal transduction with quantum theory and the collective unconscious, it seems that **beliefs and subsequent actions, may be the underlying mechanism for manifesting reality**.

There are numerous examples of people who experience spontaneous healing and unexplainable remission from chronic diseases and various health problems, without the use of allopathic medicine. Similarly, the placebo effect is a well documented phenomena accounting for belief based healing. Volumes of medical studies and scholarly articles indicate that many patients who receive the sugar pill placebo experience healing and remission from their condition, implying that their body healed because they believed they were receiving medicine that would heal them. And yet many doctors and scientists struggle to fit spontaneous remission or the placebo effect into an academic medical context.

The phenomena of extreme **Multiple Personality Disorder (Dissociative Identity Disorder) may provide clinical evidence implying that beliefs and consciousness create or impact the condition of the human body**. It has been documented that DID personality shifts can be so dramatic that the body of the person undergoes major changes in the instant that the personality shifts. For example, one of the patient's personalities is blind, and when the blind patient shifts to the other personality- that personality can instantly see. In other cases one personality has brown eyes, and the other has blue eyes, or one personality has allergic reactions to a food, and the other personality eats that food without any problems.

A New York Times archive article from June 28th, 1988, titled Probing the Enigma of Multiple Personality, shares the story of a multiple personality disorder patient who likes to drink orange juice as the personality Timmy. However, if he changes into another personality he is instantly allergic to the orange juice he's been drinking, causing him to break out in hives. What is even wilder is that if he switches back to Timmy again, the hives immediately begin to subside and heal.

Researchers have been fascinated with studying multiple personality disorder patients, like Timmy, who change physiologically when their personality makes extreme shifts.

A Washington Post article from November 24, 2015 shares the incredible story of **a woman who had been blind for 15 years, then miraculously regained her vision** when she shifted into a different personality. As she continued to shift between personalities, her vision would come and go depending on which personality was dominant at any given moment. Her ability to see was completely dependent on her psychological condition.

I feel this interaction represents the part of me that doesn't stand up for myself and chooses to be passive when I need to set boundaries. The woman that I touched inappropriately needed to have boundaries with me, and even when I knew and insisted that I was in the wrong, she tried to reassure me rather than assert appropriate boundaries. Similarly, I needed to make boundaries with the cannabis vendor, assert myself to obtain my card, and not overpay for the cannabis. Interesting to note that cannabis buds are obtained from the female plant, and that smoking buds can sometimes encourage people in being overly passive and non-assertive (that's my personal experience when I use too much cannabis, although it is generally I phenomenal medicine for many conditions).

After I left the head shop I got into a car with a woman that once worked for my parent's business in the Human Resources position. She was driving, and I was looking at the cannabis I had just got from the head shop. I was a little upset about the small amount for the large sum I had paid. I was complaining to her about the quality, quantity, and that there was hash oil soaking one of the cannabis bags. The HR lady was attempting to comfort me and convince me that everything was fine, and the cannabis looked good. I suppose that she represented the part of me that wants to soothe, pacify, and encourage positive feelings. However, this sometimes leads to sweeping things under the rug, until the rug has too much stuff under it; in which case this part of the Anima needs balance and clarity about what is in alignment and out of alignment.

However, when I originally wrote the previous paragraph about this HR lady in my dream, it was just a day or two after I had the dream. Since then, (a few weeks later) I went to my brother's house to see his newborn baby and hang out with him and his wife.

I was a little surprised to see this HR lady there when I arrived, but I knew they were all friends and that she and my brother had worked together, so it wasn't much of a surprise. However, as we all sat around chatting and holding the baby, she began to talk about her investments in the Cannabis industry in Canada. Apparently, she had invested a few thousand dollars in Canadian cannabis industry stocks, and the investments were doing very well for her. At the time of her telling me this, I didn't make the connection to my dream about her and cannabis. Its only now as I'm re-reading this chapter and editing it that I realize I dreamed about her involvement with cannabis before she told me about her cannabis stocks.

I rarely see this woman, and I have never heard her speak about cannabis or associated it with her in any way. When I do see her its usually in passing and we don't take the time to talk much outside of polite greetings. So now that I am realizing this connection between my dream about her and my waking life experience of her encouraging cannabis stock investments, I am recognizing that this dream synchronicity is also an example of a message from the collective unconscious, holomovement, or spirit, and that there is more in it for me to contemplate and unpack.

Jung talks about the importance of subjective interpretations and analyzing how a dream motif relates to the individual, depending on their personal circumstances and relation to what is being shown in the dream. For me some dreams have been mysterious and needed an expert like C.G Jung to help with analysis (although through practice I have become increasingly satisfied with my interpretations). Other dreams are very straightforward, profoundly clear, and without need of interpretation. Some dreams seem to come from a higher dimensional realm or a spiritual place that is

It was sometime in 2009 when I took Lopaka up to my dad's house to play music and hang out with a group of friends. We were driving up my dad's long ½ mile driveway when Lopaka said to me, "Benny, what is this place? I been everywhere in Kona, but never been up here. There's something about this place. Something up here, I can feel it."

"There is something up here," I verified for him, "I will show you." I didn't elaborate on what I thought it was, because I wanted to see what Lopaka would say about it, and how he would genuinely perceive it without any suggestion from me. He was quiet after I said, "I will show you," as if he was waiting for me to tell him more, or perhaps he was already imagining what it was and needed no further explanation.

It was my perception that there was a vortex located near my dad's house in the middle of the driveway. My Dad's driveway goes up a steep hill, with a coffee plantation on the left side of it, while the right side is a raw jungle forest with avocado, bamboo, ti leaf, and other plants. My Dad's house sits up at the top of the driveway. I had visited this vortex many times at night and done many mediations there. Before my awareness of vortexes, I was always attracted to this place on my dad's driveway, particularly at night. I would feel an urge to walk down to this place and meditate there. However, it seemed dark and scary, and I was often too afraid to go there. It wasn't until I learned to identify vortexes and energy overlays through meditation that I finally realized why I was so attracted to this place that also scared me. It was because **the vortex attracted spiritual activity**, and it was the spiritual activity that scared me, which happens more frequently in the evening. Paradoxically it was the spiritual activity that also attracted me.

I took Lopaka to the place on my dad's driveway where the vortex is. I didn't say a word to him about my meditations with spirits or what I previously did there. I got out of the car and walked to the place where I would normally stand during the meditation. I began to imagine it happening the way it normally did. A line of spirits would approach the vortex from east to west, or from uphill to downhill. The vortex would be directly in front of me as I was facing uphill or east. As the spirits approached they would go up through the vortex and into the sky guiding them to the higher dimensional realm of Christ consciousness and off the planet. I imagined them ascending through this vertical vortex pillar of light right in front of my face.

Lopaka was standing next to me and he said excitedly while pointing his finger at the vortex, "Benny! You see dat! They're right in front of you brah! They're coming down in a line and moving up into the sky right in front of you!"

Upon hearing him say that, tears began to roll down my cheeks. I didn't speak or respond. I continued the meditation because I didn't want to interrupt the process of ascension. I took it very seriously. However, it was very emotional to hear his validation, to hear him describe to me exactly what I was doing, without me having said a word to him about it.

Even after his validation I still didn't share with him about my process or anything regarding my thoughts about it. Sometimes I regret not sharing with him about what I was doing, which would have validated for him what he was seeing. I could have given him that validation the way he gave it to me. Yet I still didn't trust anyone enough to share my process at that time, as it's a very vulnerable thing to do. I didn't want him sharing my deepest secrets at that time trained to be salespeople for big pharma. Meanwhile aspiring students unwittingly acquire half a million dollars of medical school debt, which provides them with a large incentive to stay the pharmaceutical course, stick to their training, and follow the path laid out for them. Hence, natural alternatives, diet and lifestyle, herbs and supplements, and mental/emotional factors, can appear like a threat to the medical-ego-belief-structure-buy-in of recently graduated medical students.

This is painfully obvious by the increase of chronic conditions in America, such as type two Diabetes, Heart Disease, Cancer, and Autoimmune conditions. These conditions are generally known to be caused by diet, lifestyle, and toxicity, as demonstrated by scholarly articles or even plain old-fashioned common sense. And yet the medical industry continues to treat these conditions with pharmaceutical drugs. Factually speaking, all of these conditions combined impact more than one half of the American population.

The Federal government and World Health Organization have published lists of toxic chemicals that they know cause cancer. And yet when a person is diagnosed with cancer they are not treated by the medical industry as if they may need to detoxify or chelate these toxic chemicals from their body. There are a variety of tests to determine toxicity, and a variety of detoxification methods, and yet none of these are a legal treatment for dealing with cancer (although clinics in Mexico, like the Gerson clinic, provide detoxification treatments for cancer). In fact, the common medical treatment is to add more toxic chemicals to the body. And while I've heard many times people say, "we're all gonna die of something anyway," after watching my father horrifically suffer through cancer and chemo treatments, I can imagine much more gentle and natural ways to pass.

As I continued to struggle with chronic infections into my teenage years, I would learn at the age of 17 that my Dad was diagnosed with Multiple Myeloma, commonly known as Bone Marrow Cancer. This had a huge impact on my family and myself. And while I watched my Dad's body breakdown and transform from the muscular and healthy body I had always known, into something skeletal and sickly, there was a silver lining that was to come.

My Dad initially went through chemotherapy until he got to a point where his white blood cell count would not go back up. The doctors said they could not continue with chemo because his white blood cells were at a dangerously low level. Instead they gave him a death sentence of less than two years and sent him home with experimental drugs.

However, my Dad did not choose to die. When I say choose, I mean that I feel he made a conscious choice to live. I watched him change his beliefs. I saw him become a spiritual person for the first time in my life. He didn't choose a religion, because he was too well studied on the history of organized religions, but rather he chose to pray every day to a higher power. In his prayer he gave thanks for his life and his health. My Dad quit practicing law, a job that stressed him out, and he took up writing a book. He apologized for much of his previously harsh behaviors and changed much of his attitude toward people and life in general. It was during this time of his life that my Dad tested out as cancer free and went into remission.

Unfortunately, after a few years of writing, my Dad's book was never published, and when he ran out of money he started practicing law again. It was at this time that I saw my Dad's cancer come back. He received low level chemo treatments once a week for the next decade or so, that he could live and work through without losing his quality of life. My Dad eventually passed away seventeen years after his initial diagnosis, fifteen years longer than the doctors gave him to live. His final cause of death was intense chemo poisoning that caused liver failure, kidney failure, and congestive heart failure. It was a ruthless five consecutive days of chemotherapy that poisoned him, causing two months of awful suffering before he finally chose to quit dialysis and let himself pass on.

However, the health lessons I learned from my Dad's experience are priceless. I watched my Dad transform his life, change his actions and beliefs, and go into a spontaneous remission. After a few years I watched him go back to some of his old patterns, like practicing law, and at this time I saw his cancer return. I saw the mechanism of dis-ease ebb and flow like a tide that I believe he controlled, consciously or unconsciously, by his beliefs and actions. I feel blessed to have been able to witness that process and apply my Dad's lessons to my own life.

In my health and healing journey I have discovered that the following themes are crucial factors involving human health: Diet, Lifestyle, Exercise, and Beliefs.

Diet was the first thing I really connected to my health. As I became spiritual and more conscious in general, I became more conscious of my diet and how it was impacting my health. I have gone through many phases of dietary consciousness, and I can't say for certain that there is one diet that is best for everyone. People have different dietary needs depending on their lifestyle, exercise levels, toxicity, weight, health condition, etc.

However, I feel there are some common dietary threads that can apply to almost everyone. Ultimately my goal is to stay non-toxic and nutritionally efficient. I don't want to pollute my trillions of cells with toxins that will cause epi-genetic defects and mutations, and I want to obtain the maximum amount of nutrition out of my food choices that will optimize my cellular functions.

The most nutritionally dense foods are also the highest vibrational foods. These are sprouts, micro-greens, and blue-green algae (Spirulina and Chlorella). Other highly nutritious whole foods are vibrantly colorful such as cruciferous vegetables, beets, carrots, berries, herbs, coconuts, etc.

The human body is physically created by the water we drink, the food we consume, and the air we breathe. These three factors are crucial to human health. If our air, food, or water is polluted, then the human body is absorbing toxic pollution and forcing the cells to have a detoxification response. What are called phase 1 and 2 detoxification, can eliminate many toxins in the human body, and yet these detox processes cannot be taken for granted. Some people are born with epigenetic defects that limit their ability to detoxify. Other people have been bombarded with a lifetime of toxins before they have reached adulthood, and therefore have depleted their detox ability. Either way, if the goal is optimum health, then it is important that we choose non-toxic as much as possible.

There are also ways to improve detoxification in the body. However, I do not suggest using this as a tool to balance toxic choices. That will catch up with you. However, for those who want to detoxify and stay on top of their detox game, there is a simple, safe, and healthful way to constantly detox using MSM and Vitamin C. When taken together, these two supplements feed the body's collagens while safely removing toxins. Collagens are the most abundant protein type in the human body, and they are crucial to every part of the body. 3,000-5,000mg each of MSM and Vitamin C, three times per

I have found that consistent exercise is crucial to energy, mood, and muscle strength and flexibility. After running barefoot on the beach, stretching my legs and hips, and going for a long swim in the ocean, I feel amazing. I like to exercise first thing in the morning before eating any food. I drink 32oz of water first, and then exercise, which shakes up the lymphatic system allowing detoxification and increased circulation. When I finish exercising I make sure to begin my metabolic cycle with highly nutritious organic food that works for my body type. This exercise and diet system, combined with a regular yoga practice, is optimum.

Other important health factors involve lifestyle product choices such as toothpaste, soap, deodorant, cleaning products, and general body and beauty products. Toxins absorbed through human skin can be worse than toxins that are eaten in food, because food toxins can at least be detoxified by the liver and kidneys. Toxic body products can cause a wide range of health problems, and I find that I feel better when I use organic non-toxic products while also minimizing my need for such products.

Toxic household cleaning products have been shown to increase VOC's and other airborne toxins in the home. There are organic laundry soaps, but I find that just using a ¼ cup of Borax and a few drops of lavender essential oil fulfills my laundry needs. For dish soap I use Dr. Bronner's peppermint soap, although I find many things can be washed with just water. Mopping the floors can be done with mostly water, vinegar, and/or a few drops of essential oils such as eucalyptus, tea tree, lavender, clove, cinnamon, lemon, thyme, oregano, etc.

However, belief and emotionality are perhaps the most important health and healing factors. All the right healthy foods, herbs, supplements, and non-toxic lifestyle products won't make a difference under the constant stress of negative beliefs, emotions, and the resulting hormonal responses that cause epigenetic expressions of chronic dis-ease.

The famous biologist Bruce H. Lipton, PHD, in his book The Biology of Belief, explains the correlation of genes to human health using the following analogy. Imagine your genes are like the key to your car. Your car key is correlated with driving your car because you need it to start the ignition. But you don't say that your key *causes* your car to drive from here to there, because otherwise your key could hijack your car. Ultimately you are the driver of your car.

Gene expression is similar. We have many genes that can express as health or disease, but the expression is dependent on our environment, food and substances we consume, but most importantly our own beliefs. Dr. Lipton writes:

> *Thoughts, the minds energy, directly influence*
> *how the brain controls the body's physiology.*
> *Thought "energy" can activate or inhibit the cell's*
> *function producing proteins via the mechanics*
> *of constructive and destructive interference.*

The process of changing beliefs, and imagining positive framework for people and circumstances, that is encouraging of excitement, learning, growth, and transformation, is crucially important for mental emotional health. However, diet and lifestyle factors tie back into mental health issues, suggesting the importance of a holistic health plan that is inclusive of many different health and healing modalities.

PSYCHOACTIVE

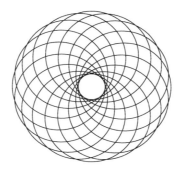

WHILE **PSYCHOACTIVE SUBSTANCES** have played a positive and helpful role in my life and spirituality, as well as a multicultural role in countless culture for thousands of years, I have experienced the American party culture misuse and abuse of substances, leading to a "bad trip" or worse. However, these substances have played an integral role in the human story and have led to some of the great cultural innovations in society. Personally, I have experienced both sides of using psychoactive substances, the positive and negative impacts, and some of the grey areas in between. Regardless, in my overall personal experience, the use of psychoactive substances has contributed to an increase of my awareness of synchronicity, spirituality, and consciousness.

The experience I write about in Chapter 1, in which I became aware of a tingling synchronicity, happened while I was under the influence of cannabis. However, the story begins earlier that day when I was completely sober. I had been sober for about a week after New Year's Eve of 2004-2005 (we had partied that night for new year's eve). I walked into Waipio valley on New Year's Day and my intention of going into the valley was to deny myself of substances and the usual societal desires, as I was attempting to understand myself on a deeper level.

This paradoxical intention of desiring not to desire, combined with being in a remote cabin in the valley, led to a heightened sense of awareness during the days to come. On the morning of the day that I would discover the tingling sensations, I saw what I perceived to be an extra sort of light located above a little bathing pool in one of the many streams in the valley. The light looked magical, as did the pool, and I got into the pool with the intent of baptizing myself. Not in the religious sense of a baptism, but rather more spiritually intent on washing away negative energy and bringing in positive spiritual energy. Noticing the light inspired my intention to experience a sort of baptism.

After emerging from the baptism pool, I saw the light a short distance away, this time over a beautiful little waterfall located upstream. I crawled through the shallow stream under a gorgeous display of moist spider webs, crawling on all fours between the webs and the water, as I didn't want to disturb the mystical webs. I thought about the web of life, and the spirit energy that connects all that is. When I reached the waterfall, I meditated on letting the water wash away the negative energy and **allowing positive 'web of life' energy** to enter my body. After emerging from the falls, I climbed up to the top of it and again saw the light in the distance upstream.

I walked upstream until I came to a large shallow radiant pool of water that had beautiful smooth flat stepping stones laid into its bottom. The stones were so perfectly connected they looked like they were intentionally placed there. I could see the light at the other side of this pool, and so I walked gently and slowly across the stones, stepping into ankle deep water, thinking and meditating on the symbolism of stepping stones and where this new light was taking me, literally and metaphorically. I remember hearing Bob Marley's lyrics playing in my head:

There's a natural mystic blowing through the air
If you listen carefully now you will hear

At the end of the pool, beyond the last stepping stone, I saw the light in a bush. It was an unreal sight to see this hedgy bush illuminated perfectly. As I approached the bush, I saw that it looked hollow inside and had grown in such a way that it looked like a brightly lit meditation chamber. Naturally I got into the hollow of the bush and proceeded to meditate. As my meditation deepened it became clear that the concept of faith and trust in the universe, god, spirit, and my aligned sense of self, was the crucial theme of following this light guided adventure.

I was still meditating in the bush when I heard and felt a rumbling on the ground. It sounded like a group of large animals. I could feel them getting closer to where I was, but because I was sitting in a bush I couldn't see where they were or what they looked like. I assumed they were horses, because Waipio is loaded with wild horses. Because I was still in meditation, I was able to observe my thoughts and see the introduction of fearful survival-based ideas come to mind like 'get up and run'. I felt and heard the rumbling of animal hooves get closer and closer. A part of me felt tantalized in wanting to get up and see what was coming. Of course, the animals eventually passed through and all felt peaceful once again.

To be fair, as I reflect on the story, although I felt afraid in that moment, I realize that it was unlikely that the horses would have run into the bush. They are perhaps more likely to stay on an easier path with less obstruction. But at that time, the approach of the sound was like an intense crescendo that began as something faint and distant, and gradually grew into a nearby uproar that felt like it almost got me. While I could have acted on leaving the bush and traveling to a certain safety, the experience felt like a synchronously timed test.

A relevant verse from the Tao Te Ching says:

One who embraces the fullness of Virtue Can
be compared to a newborn babe. Wasps and
scorpions, snakes and vipers do not sting him;
Birds of prey and fierce beasts do not seize him;

(Robert Henricks translation of the Ma-wang-tui texts, Chapter 55)

After my meditation, I left the bush and saw the light going up a nearby stream. I followed this stream only to find that it led to the back of the cabin where I was staying. My day long adventure had come to an end, and I unknowingly came full circle back to the cabin. The light had prevailed, and the synchronicity of it returning me to my cabin felt glorious and blessed. The cabin looked bright and sparkling as I approached.

Upon arrival to the cabin, I saw my friend Tobias there working around the house. His family owned the property, and it was normal for him to be there doing maintenance and whatnot. He asked me if I wanted to partake in smoking some cannabis with him. For a moment I hesitated, because of my **desire not to desire**, cannabis was something I was denying myself. However, it occurred to me that perhaps my desire to be totally substance free was also a desire and attachment.

I therefore agreed to smoke some cannabis with Tobias. Due to that choice I received a mind-expanding story that led to the most transformative experience of my life up to that point. As we smoked, Tobias told me about a Tsunami, due to a major earthquake, that had happened in Thailand just a few weeks prior. He was sharing with me that trained Elephants could sense the Tsunami coming, and how they picked up young children and took them to safety. Tobias explained that animals have senses that pick-up on natural disasters and other events. He said to me, "Humans have that ability too... We have extra senses like the elephants, but we block our awareness of it by focusing on jobs, relationships, and other human distractions."

Tobias profound statement synched up the Taoist verse that I had been contemplating, that was the impetus for my entire theme of desiring not to desire:

> *Therefore, those constantly without desires,*
> *by this means will perceive its subtlety.*

(Robert Henricks translation of the Ma-wang-tui texts, Chapter 1)

Tobias left around sunset, leaving me with a good story and good high on cannabis. It was at this time that I walked out on to the porch and sat down to meditate on the day's events. I believe the cannabis impacted my consciousness and encouraged me to dislodge myself from previously limiting belief systems while integrating these new and exciting understandings of reality. While it's entirely possible I could have done it without the influence of cannabis, the truth of the story is that I had a profound life altering spiritual event while cannabis was working on me. It was at that moment that I connected with everything in my reality and became **aware of the universe as a spiritual communication**, down to the *subtlety* of every little tingling sensation.

This was the moment that I write about in chapter 1, that brought me to the awareness of my spider sense. Everything I was experiencing in the valley up to that point, including Tobias' story and advice, led me to the realization of the depth of synchronicity. However, it was under the influence of cannabis that everything clicked, and I felt elevated to a higher state of consciousness. But the point of learning to familiarize myself with consciousness through cannabis, is to learn how to be in that state when I'm sober, without the help of the plant. If the plant is a teacher, then once the lesson is learned it doesn't need to be revisited.

Although I have had times of overindulging in cannabis, I have very little use for cannabis now at this point in my life. I keep high CBD strains on hand for various health and healing purposes, but I'm generally 99% sober in my life. As I'm writing this I would easily pass a drug test. That being said, **cannabis and other psychoactive substances can be great medicines** if used with that intent. As a society we have now come to the medical awareness that cannabis is a profoundly helpful treatment for serious seizure conditions, cancer, migraine headaches, and many other chronic health conditions.

More recently LSD, Psilocybin (Magic) Mushrooms, and DMT have been studied by psychiatrists in a therapeutic setting, with profound impacts reported after just one or two treatments with patients. In a 2017 scholarly article published in the Journal of Psychoactive Drugs (Thomas K, Malcolm B, Lastra D) the researchers write:

There were seven clinical trials that investigated psilocybin-assisted therapy as a treatment for psychiatric disorders related to anxiety, depression, and substance use. All trials demonstrated reductions in psychiatric rating scale scores or increased response and remission rates. There were large effect sizes related to improved depression and anxiety symptoms. Psilocybin may also potentially reduce alcohol or tobacco use and increase abstinence rates in addiction...

An April 2017 scholarly article written by Robin L Carhart-Harris (Neuropsychopharmacology, The Therapeutic Potential of Psychedelic Drugs: Past, Present, and Future) shares the following insights:

Since the early 1990s, there has been a steady revival of human psychedelic research: last year saw reports on the first modern brain imaging study with LSD and three separate clinical trials of psilocybin for depressive symptoms...with a focus on the development of psilocybin as a treatment for depression.

In my personal experimentation with substances I have noticed that psilocybin mushrooms, LSD, ayahuasca, DMT, and other psychoactive substances are generally non-addictive. After every experience on one of those substances, I didn't have a desire to take the substance again, but also felt like I wanted to be sober in general for at least a few weeks after. I noticed a similar trend in other friends as well. My friend's Dad used low doses of LSD to quit drinking alcohol. He had previously been an alcoholic and found that a daily half dose of LSD was enough to keep him sober. On a half hit he was able to go to work as a plumbing installation contractor. He installed significant amounts of plumbing in residential building projects in Kona on low doses of LSD!

He shared his LSD with other alcoholics he met at job sites. He was a low-key LSD distributor to people who needed to quit addictive substances. He helped many people in this way, and his funeral was packed with those who had something good to say about his help.

He had been a road man for the Native American Church. He had the responsibility of bringing peyote from one ceremony to another in various locations. At a young age he taught me that the use of psychoactive substances was not something to party with, or play around with for fun and games. He shared with me that native peoples understood that taking psychoactive substances changes you as a mental, emotional, and spiritual organism. **Therefore, it is important to meditate on the type of change you wish to experience, to be clear about your intentions, and to use the substance in a setting that allows and encourages such changes to take place.** I would come to learn that under the influence of psychoactive substances I was able to unlock myself from negative limiting beliefs, transforming my beliefs and definitions into positive expansive empowering beliefs.

DMT was one of the more powerful substances I tried that could unlock me from limiting beliefs. I was 25 years old when I tried Dimethyltryptamine (DMT) for the first time. DMT is a plant molecule extract known for facilitating consciousness expansion and "out of body" experiences. It is an endogenous molecule produced naturally by the human body and is also found in many plants. My experience with DMT gave me a sense of connection to the world, which put me on a path of **looking at reality, mother earth, and all living beings as a connected whole system.**

I was at my friend's house in Miloli'i on a little mac nut farm. Our mutual friend offered us DMT, so we walked out to a little grassy area in the yard where we sat down under the starry night sky. Just moments after smoking DMT I initially felt like the sky was crushing me into the ground. As I lay helpless in a fetal position I felt this awful dense weighted high pressure feeling. I thought about it for a moment and I remember thinking, 'well if this is what's happening there's not much I can do about it… so I might as well accept it, surrender to it, and be ok with it.'

As I surrendered to the DMT experience and accepted what was happening I soon began to lighten up. I literally felt lighter and lighter until I was sitting up straight and feeling quite good. I opened my eyes and saw energy lines everywhere. I could still see my friend's house, the mac nut orchard, and my friend sitting next to me. The only difference was that very clear lines of energy, like bright curved lightning chords, were running through everything and connecting everything to me. The energy lines coming out of my body were connecting to everything else that was around me, like a web of energetic connection. In that moment I had a very old age eastern thought epiphany, 'everything is connected.'

Just yesterday, before I started the second round of editing this chapter today, I read a passage written by Carlos Castaneda in his book The Art of Dreaming, in which he describes one of the various teachings of his Nagual benefactor Don Juan. This paragraph describes the energy lines I saw on DMT, while adding deeper conscious awareness to those lines or threads:

For such sorcerers, the most significant act of sorcery
is to see the essence of the universe. Don Juan's
version was that the sorcerers of antiquity, the first
ones to see the essence of the universe, described it
in the best manner. They said that the essence of the
universe resembles incandescent threads stretched
into infinity in every conceivable direction, luminous
filaments that are conscious of themselves in ways
impossible for the human mind to comprehend.

That initial DMT experience was about two years after the discovery of my spider sense tingling sensations. Seeing a web of energy threads connecting to everything confirmed to me that calling my intuitive synchronous tingles a "spider sense" was a fair description. Experiencing and feeling those energy threads gave me insight into how my tingling sensations mechanically operate in connection to everything else. I experienced a layer of energy that we don't normally perceive with our eyes and ears, yet could give an explanation to what people generally experience as intuition, psychic phenomena, synchronicity, and spiritual activity. We often think of these events as magical, special, or sometimes too 'out there' to talk about. But what if there was **an invisible layer of conscious energy connecting all things, that could provide a physical explanation for psychic, spiritual, and synchronous phenomena.** Perhaps what people refer to as God is not a man in the sky, but rather an energy or consciousness that permeates all that is.

We cannot see normal everyday electricity and yet we see its manifestations every time we turn on a light bulb. We know that the earth has an electromagnetic field and yet we cannot see or hear it. We know that there is energy and electricity coursing through our bodies, and yet we do not see it or generally think much of it. Science tells us that there are spectrums of light and electromagnetism that we cannot see, but that these energy fields are all around us. Radio waves, blue tooth, cellular signals, and other types of electromagnetic frequencies are all around us creating phenomenal technological abilities, and yet we do not see them transmitting. Therefore, it isn't too far-fetched to imagine that there are energy chords connecting all of us to all that is.

I cannot prove that such energy chords exist. However, when I visually experienced the idea that we are all energetically connected, it gave me a sense of clarity around the synchronous, psychic, and spiritual phenomena that I had experienced. Seeing energy lines connecting to everything like a web, planted the idea in my mind that there may be an undiscovered (or unknown to me) scientific explanation for such phenomena.

Exploring the research and ideas of quantum physicists like David Bohm or Niels Bohr, I have found further insights into the possibility that the energy lines I saw in my DMT trip were not just hallucinations or nice new age fairy tale euphemisms, but rather the way in which reality may possibly be structured as a connected whole system. As I mentioned in Chapter of 4 of this book, the idea that all physical matter primarily exist as energy waves is the foundational basis for widely accepted quantum theory. Therefore we know that we exist within a vast ocean of energy waves and frequencies, and that our **human bodies are essentially energy waves and frequencies**, and so perhaps we are all projections of a holomovement as Bohm suggests.

Regardless of the implications of quantum theory or various philosophies about the nature of reality, the experience of psychoactive substances can facilitate a feeling of connection and belonging to All That Is. In my personal experience I have made positive changes and become quite a different person through the education I have received from the use of psychoactive substances. I experience a much greater degree of calm, positivity, and clarity about what genuinely excites me. However, while some substances have certainly been helpful at times, other substances have been harmful.

I generally imagine two types of drug categories in my experience, although I'm not dogmatic about any of these and I believe they all have their proper dosage, place and time of use. That being said, I believe I can generally say that toxic addictive drugs such as pharmaceutical drugs, opiates, muscle relaxers, psychiatric drugs, alcohol, cocaine, tobacco, angel dust, meth, and white powder drugs are the types that I have seen ruin people's health, mind, and livelihood, creating nightmarish scenarios for family and friends. In contrast to that I have seen mushrooms, LSD, ayahuasca, DMT, cannabis, San Pedro cactus, kava, and other natural psychoactive substances work wonders for people's mental/emotional health, spiritual connectivity, and overall health. However, the second category of substances are not always effective and can sometimes make things much worse. **The use of plant medicines needs to be taken on a case by case basis** with certain factors taken into consideration: mental/emotional state, environment, dose, intention, appropriate substance of choice, and overall health.

I recently watched a well-made documentary about the blessed and troubled life of one of the greatest professional surfers of our time, Andy Irons. The film illustrates Andy's struggle with mental health challenges, his subsequent drug use, and ultimately a drug addiction that led to a deadly heart attack. What struck me about this film was that I could relate to some of Andy's mental/emotional issues, and the desire to take drugs as a strategy to alleviate all the busy negative thoughts running through the mind. Although I don't know exactly what its like to be in Andy's head, I could relate to some of his interviews and written notes that pertained to his mental issues.

As a child I had times in which it felt like I just wanted to turn off my mind. Sometimes multiple voices chatting in my head all at once scared and confused me, making it hard to focus and enjoy the moment. I manifested psychological tics that concerned my mom and subsequently landed me in therapy at a very young age. However, my therapist only recommended the amphetamine drug Ritalin, which is a very toxic and addictive form of speed similar to meth. My mom was smart enough to decline drug use for me, but she wasn't given any alternative positive tools to help me either.

This mental emotional condition stuck with me until high school. I had been generally afraid of drug use up until 9th grade when I first tried cannabis. At that timer cannabis was way too intense for me, and although my friends continued to experiment with it, I personally didn't like the way it made me feel. However, when I tried LSD and Mushrooms in small doses, I found something that finally shut my mind off and brought me into the moment. For the first time in my life I felt free from my own mind.

It took a lot of experimentation with LSD and Mushrooms before figuring out that I preferred small doses accompanied with daytime physical activity, like going for a hike, skateboarding, or playing in the ocean. These times of proper self-medication increasingly brought my mind into a healthier state by facing and overcoming my fears, connecting me to nature, myself, and spirit. However, I also experienced times of unhealthy self-medication, using way too much mushrooms and LSD in one sitting, or drinking alcohol (the true gateway drug) which sometimes led to experimenting with cocaine, opiates, and pharmaceuticals.

The unhealthy addictive side of drug use is not without cause. People turn to drugs as a form of escapism when they don't have the tools to manage their mental emotional issues, past trauma, and spiritual void. **When the personality becomes fragmented and doesn't know how to attain holistic reconciliation, drug addiction can become a negative strategy that is unhealthfully employed, leading to increased disconnection.**

It is important that all substances are used properly, obtaining the appropriate substance and applying it in small doses, with the intent of regaining mental and emotional stability. However, drugs are not always necessary. Meditation, hypnosis, and other forms of subconscious reprogramming can be very beneficial. These practices can also be applied in conjunction with micro-dosing psychoactive drugs, to help with the process of becoming aware of and unlocking from negative beliefs that are hidden deep in the subconscious.

Ancient cultures recognized the ability of psychoactive plants to aid and assist in achieving mental/emotional healing and progress. Doctors and scholars are now discovering some of these amazing qualities in a clinical setting. It is important that our culture recognizes the medicinal value and appropriate use of drugs, clearly identifying the role of psychoactive substances in health and healing. With the right kind of guidance, education, and environment, we can use substances as they are intended to be used, while avoiding the misuse of substances that can become a negative experience or an unhealthy addiction.

ADDICTION

LIKE MOST PEOPLE, I have experienced various manifestations of addiction. My personal experience ranges from binging on junk foods and television as a young child, to alcohol and drug abuse as a young adult. I have even found myself in versions of spiritual extremism that became an unhealthy addiction. Addiction can take many forms: the diabetic that refuses to change their diet, the millennial that can't stop looking at their phone, the sex addict that feels lonely and unloved, the cigarette smoker that develops lung cancer, the workaholic that doesn't spend quality time with their family or children, the incessant talker that is constantly looking for validation, the ruthless businessman who is unethical in his motivation to make as much money as possible, the adrenaline junkie seeking the next thrill ride; all of these addictive personality types may have a common underlying cause.

While the drug of choice may be different, as illustrated by the manifestations described in the previous paragraph, addictive behaviors often develop from an underlying strategy of attempting to fulfill an unmet need and to escape from the reality or environment that causes or perpetuates the unmet need. The desire to escape something, to feel validated, and ultimately the need to receive empathy and understanding; without a healthy strategy to meet those needs, often results in some type of substance abuse. However, with a general lack of self-awareness, most of us don't realize that the reason we abuse substances, people, and ourselves, is that we have unmet needs and negative strategy belief systems that can never fulfill those needs.

Erich Fromm describes addictive behaviors in terms of rebellion and resistance beginning in childhood. Fromm writes, "The tendency to grow in terms of their own nature is common to all living beings." Unfortunately, in an unbalanced competitive consumer culture, "The growing person is forced to give up most of his or her autonomous, genuine desires and interests, and his or her own will, and to adopt a will and desires and feelings that are not autonomous but superimposed by social patterns of thought and feeling." Fromm goes on to explain that unnatural and unhealthy societal limitations cause the child to have feelings of rebellion and resistance. Although rebellion can manifest in healthy productive ways, it can often be self-destructive, violent, and unhealthy, as is true for addictive choices. Fromm cites a paper from David E. Schecter in which he summarizes, "All data indicate that heteronomous (subject to the rule of another) interference with the child's and the later persons growth process is the deepest root of mental pathology, especially of destructiveness."

Fromm therefore advocates for a type of freedom, but he warns that, "Freedom does not mean freedom from all guiding principles. It means the freedom to grow according to the laws of the structure of human existence (autonomous restrictions). It means obedience to the laws that govern optimal human development."

The critical thinking reader may question at this point: How do we know which laws govern optimal human development?

I would argue that we assess it on a case by case basis mixed with some common general themes, encouraging individuality within whole system values and responsibility. For example, each child feels their own individual excitement, and it can lead them from one pathway of progress, learning, and experience, into further expanded pathways of excitement as they continue to grow and evolve. However, the underlying general theme is the encouragement of excitement in a healthy, loving, conscious way. In this way the child feels the freedom to explore their genuine excitement within reasonable boundaries of safety and health. Healthy boundaries involve a whole system perspective that includes caring for others and sharing one's unique gifts in a mutually helpful way, while respecting the sustainable management and distribution of planetary ecological resources.

If children can learn to live with genuine excitement and responsibility, then perhaps they won't crave materialism, substances, and escapism to fill the void of not living a meaningful exciting life. **When a person feels genuinely excited about something, there isn't a need for a drug, substance, or object to create a false sense of excitement that is a cover up or escape from not being one's true self; or to numb the pain of living in a cruel or hostile environment.**

Echoing the idea of trauma, Dr. Bruce K. Alexander, Professor Emeritus, describes how psychologists performed drug addiction experiments on rats in the 1960's:

> ... *This required tethering the rat to the ceiling of the box with tubing and surgically implanting a needle, or catheter, into their jugular veins. The drug passed through the tube and the needle into the rats' bloodstreams almost instantaneously when they pushed the lever. It reached their brains moments later.*

> *Under appropriate conditions, rats would press the lever often enough to consume large amounts of heroin, morphine, amphetamine, cocaine, and other drugs in this situation.*

However, it occurred to Alexander that these experiments were not at all a realistic model for drug addiction because the rats had been placed in an unnatural environment under cruel conditions. He learned that rats are naturally very social and industrious creatures who enjoy open space and sexual activity. Placing them in solitary confinement and tethered to a ceiling with a needle and catheter inserted into the body, might be similar to placing a human being in a cruel and unnatural environment.

This epiphany was the inspiration for Bruce K. Alexander's famous experiment known as Rat Park, in which Alexander and his team designed a sort of utopian rat world with plenty of space, food, water, and other rats to socialize and mate with. He writes about the experiment results on his website @brucekalexander.com:

> *We ran several experiments comparing the drug consumption of rats in Rat Park with rats in solitary*

confinement in regular laboratory cages. In virtually every experiment, the rats in solitary confinement consumed more drug solution, by every measure we could devise. And not just a little more. A lot more.

Alexander's experiments with rats may provide insight into the role that cruelty, trauma, and an unnatural environment play in human drug addiction. The famous addiction specialist Dr. Gabor Mate, in a podcast interview with Russel Brand (Under The Skin Episode #53) echoes the idea that trauma is the root cause of addiction. The greater severity of trauma a person experiences, the greater the addiction.

In the previous chapter I refer to the story of Andy Irons, the professional surfer whose drug addiction eventually led to a tragic heart attack. Andy had a mental emotional condition, that began in his early childhood, described by psychologists interviewed in the documentary about his life. At times he could channel his desire to escape his condition into the best competition surfing in the world, winning three consecutive world titles. At his worst, he was addicted to various drugs that disabled his ability to compete in surf contests and caused problems in his personal life. I explained previously how I could relate to Andy's story, and his description of a mind that he just wanted to turn off so that he could feel a sense of peace.

In my own childhood I experienced a similar type of chatty very busy mind accompanied with pain and fear, that made it difficult to pay attention in school and in personal conversations. I would often escape from my mind with creative projects, athletics, television and video games. However, these distractions didn't take away the root of the problem. For Andy Irons, his healthy escape was surfing, and it was such a passionate distraction that he became one of the most legendary surfers of all time. His negative escape was drugs and partying, and unfortunately that was his downfall.

The problem with escapism, even positive distractions, is that they don't address the foundational mechanism that is causing the mental emotional problem. Positive escapism is only good while the person is active in that distraction. Andy couldn't stay surfing in the ocean all day and night 24/7. Realistically there isn't any escape that can keep a person constantly distracted from their negative subconscious programming.

Finding the tingling sensation communication for me was like Andy finding his surfing. I found excitement, peace, comfort, and ease in this new way of life. However, I wanted to feel that way all the time, without confronting foundational mental emotional issues that had been with me since childhood. I became obsessed and addicted to following and focusing on this tingling sensation. It became my greatest escape, because I could apply and follow it in everything I was doing at every moment. Although it manifested very real magical synchronicities and profound experiences, I also experienced a great deal of negative synchronicity.

I experienced how my subconscious programming, childhood fear, trauma, and bad communication strategies would surface and cause disruptions in my synchronous flow. Rather than search for the negative beliefs and definitions that these behaviors were rooted in, I would justify my behavior by the tingling synchronous sage-like profound path I was experiencing that seemed infallible. I would come to later understand that this thinking was a delusional fallacy, and that although the synchronicity was real, and although I could have very real profound experiences following my tingling sensations and other mystic practices, I was delusional in thinking that I was justified and righteous in the face of manifesting negative synchronicity, negative emotional states, and dark side manifestations due to the negative programs still active in my subconscious.

I had to repeat the same frustrating negative patterns for many years before I finally humbled myself and came to the realization that I was responsible for the "bad" experiences manifesting in my life. That doesn't mean I take responsibility for the negative actions of others, or the corrupt institutions of government and economy, but I do take responsibility for my emotions and my ability to respond to life in a positive or sometimes neutral way regardless of what life is giving me.

When I feel emotionally triggered; upset, frustrated, angry, anxious, sad, violent, or depressed, I take a moment to evaluate the underlying negative beliefs that are generating the emotions. When I find the injured part of my subconscious that is surfacing with those emotions, I give that part of myself a new positive definition about that aspect of my relationship to whatever triggered me. Through this process I have been increasingly more at ease, and able to manifest a more positive relationship with myself in which I don't engage in escapism and distractions.

I still have a relationship with substances, intimacy, and spirituality, but I have transformed those relationships into something positive and healthful. For example, the relationship I have with my wife isn't centered around an addiction to intimacy. We aren't using one another to fill a void or distract ourselves from the pain of our subconscious. In fact, when we emotionally trigger each other, we both allow ourselves to take the time to meditate on what part of ourselves feels triggered, and how we can redefine that aspect of ourselves in a way that is in alignment with love, peace, excitement, and the essence of the soul. We don't need each other to be happy, but rather we add to one another's independent self-sufficient excitement and happiness.

I now only use substances very infrequently and mostly medicinally. For example, my wife's best friend was visiting us last night, and she opened a bottle of red wine. I tasted the wine while I was cooking a healthy meal, and I commented on the flavor and enjoyed the conversation around it. But I know that the sweetness of wine isn't aligned with my personal health choices, so I didn't drink a glass of it. My body communicates to me that organic vodka in very small amounts is much better for me, and especially when combined with herbal adaptogens. I pulled out a homemade tincture of Chaga, Ashwagandha, and Astragalus, that had been extracting in a jar of organic vodka. I took about ½ ounce of the tincture and applied it to about an ounce of organic, mixed in a small glass with ice cubes, to make a healthful hard liquor shot. This gave me the ability to have a drink with my girlfriend and her best friend, but in a moderate healthy way.

Spiritually I stopped relying on my tingling sensations for every little detail of my life. Instead **I follow my feelings of genuine excitement, rather than looking for what society tells me to be excited about.** I still notice when my tingling sensations are pointing to a synchronicity or offering guidance, and I am often excited to communicate with my tingling sensations in conjunction with my overall path of excitement. At the beginning of my spider sense path I followed my tingling sensations to such an extreme point, that I was literally asking for guidance with every little detail of everything I did. Eventually I realized that it wasn't always working, because I wasn't meant to do it in that way. My life and health were not sustainable at that time, because the point of life on earth is to live it, and not to ask permission for every little detail. Following my highest excitement is an indication that I'm on the path of what my soul wants to experience, but if I stop and ask for instruction every step of the way, then I may miss out on enjoying the actual experience-which is precisely the point of life- to be in-joy.

Addiction and extremism of any kind can lead to suffering. My personal path of healing from addiction has been the most successful when I'm striving for alignment with my soul and following the feeling of excitement. **Mining and transforming my subconscious programming and negative/limiting belief systems, through various types of meditations, has been crucial to discovering genuine alignment and unfiltered excitement**. To do this I have had to be brutally honest in the way I communicate with myself and others. I must be willing to look at the deepest painful fragments of my subconscious mind. I have cried deeply in meditations and discovered great healing by inviting my spirit guides to help with redefining my subconscious programming.

I believe that we all share the ability to transform anything in our lives that is relevant to our health and healing. How I communicate with myself is crucially important to discovering who I am, why I am here, and what excites me about life. Through mediation and open self-communication, I have been able to overcome many types of addiction, while finding and feeling the path of excitement that is in alignment with spirit and whole system responsibility.

COMMUNICATION

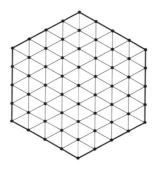

THE REALIZATION THAT EVERYTHING in my reality is communicating something to me, was a profound life changing discovery that led to my interpretation of the tingling sensations on my body as a meaningful communication from spirit. Therefore, it follows that every healing experience and positive emotional response communicates to me that I am in alignment with spirit. Likewise, every pain, illness, and negative emotional experience is a communicative indication of where I am out of alignment with spirit. By viewing my emotional and physical health status as a communication from spirit, I am always empowered to improve my reality, health, and overall wellness.

Jung defined Synchronicity as "a meaningful coincidence". I like Jung's definition as a basic starting point. From my perspective synchronicity is an intelligent communication that is reflective of the vibrational hologram function of reality. In other words, the reality

I find myself in is a reflection of the vibrational frequency I most strongly give off. Communication from a vibrational frequency perspective is perhaps a quantum mechanics description of karma, or the idea that what I put out energetically is what I get back.

When I notice synchronicity, it is because I am increasingly aware of the reflective communication that is happening all the time. I don't believe that spirit just pops in occasionally to show me a meaningful coincidence, but rather that **spirit is always present and connected to the entirety of reality; displaying, projecting, and being reality as a form of reflective communication**. The awareness of a meaningful coincidence gives us a tip or an indication that there is a spiritual communication happening, while the depth of synchronicity involves the greater awareness of spiritual communication functioning as a constant state of synchronism. In this philosophy, essentially everything is connected and constantly communicating.

The importance of communication cannot be overstated. It is paramount to every type of relationship. The relationships I propagate with other people, with great spirit, with my subconscious mind, with my soul; every relationship depends on communication. Unfortunately, we are generally not educated in public schools or in society at large on how to communicate effectively, in a way that increases mental emotional alignment, peace, excitement, and clarity. However, there are resources available that encourage positive helpful communication in a variety of healthful ways.

The problem (for the corporate and political oligarchy) with teaching positive non-violent communication in schools, is that it could potentially dismantle and reframe our education system, economy, and political structure. If children were taught to identify their true feelings and needs, and to peacefully communicate those feelings and needs to teachers and other students, the school would likely make a radical shift into a different type of educating style. The result could produce a **lack of violence that would decrease the desire for military and police, creating a massive reduction in war and prison profiteering.**

As for schools, children naturally have a need to be very physically active. It is therefore unnatural and somewhat torturous for a child to have to sit at a desk for many hours of each day, quietly writing, reading, and physically subdued. This style of spirit-breaking education may prepare the child for the workforce, or college, but it doesn't teach them about who they are or how to propagate and communicate their god given gifts.

The great educator, philosopher, and author, Paulo Freire, illustrates the problems with our education system in a model he calls the "banking concept" of education, in which students are merely viewed as empty "receptacles" to be filled with "deposits" of information.

Freire believed that ultimately the banking model of education contained deposits of information that were too isolated and detached from the whole of reality, and too often contradictory. He predicted that the oppressive educating style of "depositing" information into obedient student-like "receptacles" would ultimately lead to students seeking their own liberation. The desire for liberation is apparent in many schools with children who are diagnosed with ADD and ADHD as a result of their resistance to oppression. I would argue that the current public school system at large is a form of emotionally traumatic child abuse.

As a child I was diagnosed with Attention Deficit Hyperactive Disorder; based on a one hour questionnaire evaluation and recommendation from my school teacher. The oppression of the school system wasn't in question, but rather my desire to be free and active in my education was regarded as a disorder. However, it was never a problem for me to focus and study in my areas of interest, or when I would feel genuinely excited about a subject. I simply found public school too boring, slow, and inactive; lacking real life context and often not challenging or interesting enough to hold my attention.

Fortunately my mom had the wisdom to decline pharmaceutical amphetamine drugs; prescribed as a means to subdue my natural resistance to brainwashing. I would later find my spiritual path and come to understand myself in relation to current public education. However, the process of spiritual discovery, identifying my genuine identity, and unlearning years of oppressive education wasn't an easy walk in the park. Therefore, I find it personally and socially important to prevent the type of communication and pedagogy that encourages oppression; as we access the natural growth and evolution of individual human beings through positive foundational communication methods.

Education is a strong form of communication. The way we educate our children encourages values, skills, and connections. Therefore, how do we educate in a way that increases overall health and happiness?

Having two kids of my own, I certainly believe in communicating healthy boundaries to children. Part of our job as parents is to give our children reasonable guidance while encouraging their gifts, talents, passions and excitement about life. However, when we are not with our children, we rely on the school system to provide boundaries and education.

positive effective strategies to meet those needs, health and healing has taken place. When I have imagined communicating my needs to the spirit of Christ and asked for guidance on aligned effective strategies to meet those needs, I have received profoundly helpful answers in my meditations.

The idea that spirit is constantly communicating with me, and that reality is reflecting my choices and beliefs back to me, makes communication profoundly important. One could say that communication is the essence of life. Therefore, **communicating with *the depth of synchronicity* adds an exciting layer of magical interactions to daily life.**

We can communicate to our public-school systems that our children need to be active and excited about school, learning how to express their unique gifts and talents, alongside teachers that understand, teach and employ non-violent communication strategies. And perhaps, we can communicate to the homeless that they are infinite indestructible souls having a human experience, and that they are powerful beyond their imagination.

Everyone on the planet has the need for safety, abundance, shelter, comfort, nutrition, love, peace, and excitement. If we can break down the enemy image and see one another's universal needs and feelings, perhaps we can work together to develop whole system strategies that will lead to world peace.

COOPERATION

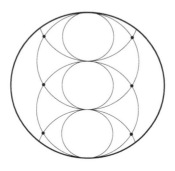

It is only because he does not compete that, therefore,
no one is able to compete with him.

– Te-Tao Ching, Chapter 22, Robert Henricks Translation

Darwin's theory of evolution was developed with the idea of competition and the survival of the fittest. This idea that competition leads to evolution, prosperity, and innovation, has been driven into us as the foundational model for buying into a pseudo capitalist system. However, this system based on competition has been wrought with war, crime, poverty, and tragedy. Biologically speaking, Darwin's ideas only speak to a portion of how evolution works. We have a multitude of examples that the success of species depends more on cooperation rather than competition.

It is first important to note that we don't have a strictly competitive capitalist socio/political/economic system; rather more of a socialist oligarchy as a result of federal government intervention and favoritism toward a multinational corporate agenda that enriches the dominance of the elite. A federal government made up of representatives whose presidential, congress, and senate campaigns are financially sponsored by the corporate oligarchy, inevitably results in politicians employing an elitist agenda ripe with conflicts of interest. Here we see a form of cooperation at the highest levels of government, leading to a favorable outcome for the elite oligarchy. Meanwhile our media and education systems are still encouraging ideas and debates about capitalism, speaking as if we live in a free market competition based system. Ultimately it appears more like the general population is led to compete with one another within the confines of many rules and laws, while the world's wealthiest people cooperate, legislate, and conspire to increase their collective wealth and dominance like a syndicate cartel.

However, the problem with a purely competitive economic system is that it encourages desperation. When the livelihood of a person's family and community depends on outcompeting their neighbor, an unnatural desperation can occur that forces unhealthy competition. On the contrary, **friendly competition does not involve life or death, wealth or poverty, health or disease; intense life impacting results**. However, the theory of capitalism and survival of the fittest require that winners will live on with opportunities for greater wealth and increased livelihood, while losers may lose everything. High stakes undoubtedly encourage a dog eat dog mentality.

We can look at models of ancient cultures that shared resources and worked together to procure their abundance. In these communities everyone had the opportunity to build a home, hunt or gather food, and create tools. Land and resources were not so privatized and therefore people were not dependent on being successful within a system that provides their abundance in exchange for labor. In many ancient cultures people had the opportunity to meet their own basic needs, having access to the earth's natural abundance that is the birthright of every human on the planet. In this model there was no illusion of scarcity that comes from the privatization of resources.

Meeting peoples basic needs encourages cooperation, industrious activity, and technological development. When Captain Cook discovered the Hawaiian people and their culture, he wrote that they were the most industrious people he had ever come across, and their advancements in agriculture were astounding. The ancient Hawaiians (Kanaka Maoli) were not in a private property system. They worked together utilizing shared land and resources. Each person's skills, talents, and gifts were identified at a young age, and that person would apprentice under the elder who was skilled in that field. For example, if a young child showed interest in fishing, stars, and ocean activity, that child would apprentice under a series of navigators that would pass on their skills in canoe building, fishing, and navigation by stars, ocean currents, weather, and wave swells.

We have been duped into thinking that without competition there is no motivation to achieve or be successful. What we see is the exact opposite. Without cooperation success is impossible. The apprentice and the teacher must cooperate for the education of skills and such to be passed on. A family must cooperate for there to be harmony and functionality. The community must cooperate for the safety, security, and abundance of all.

In this example, it is self-evident that our global socio/political/economic system encourages unhealthy unbalanced forms of competition that inevitably lead to dangerous weapons, environmental pollution, mental disorders, physical illness, and disintegration of family, community and society. By ensuring that everyone can provide for their own basic needs such as housing, food, and water, society can then have fun with healthy forms of competition, rather than systems that cause dependency and economic vulnerability that lead to desperation, violence, and criminal acts.

The famous biologist Bruce Lipton, in his book The Biology of Belief, describes the evolution of life on planet earth in the context of cooperation. For 2.75 billion years, the only life on earth were single-celled organisms like bacteria, algae, and amoeba-like protozoa. Around 750 million years ago, some of these cells got together and formed a community of multicellular organisms. In doing so, cells gained greater awareness of the environment, increased efficiency, and greater chance of survival when they worked together in complex communities we now call plants and animals. **The cooperation of cells working together is the basis of biological life and evolution.**

Cooperation is not just a nice ideal, it is the basis for a functioning human body made of trillions of cooperating cells. When our cells are not cooperating, we manifest diseases like cancer and autoimmune conditions. When the bodies trillions of cells work together like a perfect harmonic symphony, we have perfect health. It seems logical then that we could apply this notion of cooperation to our communities, culture, spirituality, and global civilization.

However, cooperation cannot be forced. Coercion is not cooperation, but rather a form of slavery, exemplified by totalitarian forms of pseudo-communism. If I was a conspiracy theorist I might wonder if the terms communism and capitalism have been mutated and perverted, perhaps to market division between groups, enhancing the political agenda of the military industrial complex? True communism is rooted in the value of a cooperative community, encouraging the idea that people will want to voluntarily work together to make life more wonderful.

Robert Henricks translation of the Tao, Chapter 3, provides some insight:

> *By not elevating the worthy, you bring it*
> *about that people will not compete.*

> *By not valuing goods that are hard to obtain, you*
> *bring it about that people will not act like thieves.*

> *By not displaying the desirable, you bring it*
> *about that people will not be confused.*

We have countless examples of cultures who operated on cooperation, community, and equality. Unfortunately, many of them have been colonized and genocide by U.S. and European imperialism. However, there are still a few examples we can look to in modern times. One such culture, the Kogi, are a civilization in Colombia, who live in the Sierra Nevada mountains, untouched by Spanish imperialism. Their culture experiences little to no murder, rape, or violent disputes. They have no poverty or wealth inequality. There is no homelessness. They generally live **peaceful, comfortable, abundant communal lives in harmony with the earth.**

A BBC documentary about the Kogi reveals that they function as a spiritually guided culture. Their shamanic elders, called Mamas, are the leaders of the culture. The Mamas organize the men and women to do various tasks such as planting and harvesting, house building, and crafting, in which the men and women work together until the task is complete. The Mamas do not live a privileged life of luxury above the common people. Their housing, amenities, and freedoms are similar to those of the common people. Their lives are simple, but beautiful and peaceful. The Mamas are more like respected guides, rather than bosses.

One of the great thinkers of our time, Charles Eisenstein, writes about various indigenous groups who share a common gifting culture. In his book **Sacred Economics,** Eisenstein tells the story of a seemingly peculiar culture in which the wealthiest person in the tribe is determined by who shares the most with others. However alien the concept may seem to a consumer economist, the value of sharing and gifting is at the root of western values, customs, and traditions.

However, Eisenstein's genius is that he connects the practical application of the gift sharing culture in contrast to an unsustainable monetary system that causes constant inflation, environmental destruction, and community disintegration. The gifting culture respects and harmonizes with the laws of nature; in which everything has a lifespan and eventual decomposition. The following excerpt is just a small sample summarizing his brilliant assessment:

>*...Over time, giving and receiving must be in balance.*
>*The internalization of ecological costs ensures that we*
>*will take no more from earth than we can give...*

...Gifts circulate rather than accumulate.
Decaying currency ensures that wealth remains
a function of flow rather than of owning...

The problem with money is that it does not decompose and its lifespan is infinite; allowing for the hoarding of wealth and hierarchical dominance. The federal reserve monetary system is perhaps the root cause of inflammatory economics. The Fed charges interest on every dollar that the U.S Government borrows; creating constant inflation. The less tax revenue, the more the federal government borrows money from the federal reserve (a private bank), which increases inflation and devalues peoples purchasing power; effecting the population like a tax. Inflation causes a systemic devaluing of the currency making ordinary people work more for less abundance. Meanwhile the majority of government revenue is spent on war and military operations enriching the pockets of military contractors.

Would we not want to trade our war, poverty, inequality, and suffering, for a simple, abundant, peaceful life?

There are many examples of cultures with simple effective technology, yet everlasting peace and abundance. It seems that **their advancements in spirituality, cooperation, love, and peace have been prioritized over technological advancements**.

The great scholar Howard Zinn, in his book The Peoples History of the United States, tells the story of Christopher Columbus through the words of Columbus' journaling and letters, and the writings of people that were there at the time of his arrival to the island of what we now call Haiti. When Columbus first arrived he discovered millions of Arawak people already living there. He described the Arawak as exceedingly peaceful and non-violent. Columbus felt that they were "naïve" because they would give him whatever food and supplies he asked for. He wrote that he could dominate the entire island with just fifty men on horseback, and that they would do so in the name of God. In the following years, a desperation and frenzy to find gold drove Columbus and the Spanish to genocide an estimated 6 million Arawak Indians, replacing them with African slaves and plantations.

In this example we see **the beauty of cooperation and non-violence as expressed by the Arawak people, and the contrast of maniacal competition portrayed by Columbus' and the Spaniards'**. Unfortunately, their imperial violent competition for resources mentality destroyed the peaceful Arawak. In the latter example we see that perhaps Darwin made a point, that competition and survival of the fittest would win at the end of the day (if the idea of winning involves murder, rape, and genocide). However, there is something about violence, murder, and genocide, that doesn't sit right with the human spirit. If these things can be done to one group, what is to stop the same type of violence from happening to us? Seeing one group of people murdered, brings up the fear and concern for our own safety; violence is unhealthy and unsustainable, while it runs the risk of human extinction. And of course, we all know the golden rule: *treat others how you wish to be treated.*

There are two thoughts on how to deal with the concern of violent imperialism. One thought, which is typical of western and American ethnocentrism, is that we must become militarily superior so that no other group of people can conquer us by force. One problem with this idea is that it only protects the wealthy and privileged group of society. The disenfranchised working classes still end up fighting the wars, going into battle, and doing the heavy lifting. Even if a soldier comes home in one piece, he or she often has PTSD trauma or a physical injury that makes it difficult to reintegrate into civilian society.

War is a profitable business. The corporations who sell weapons, vessels, and supplies, or extract resources from around the world, need war for their business to continue. The business incentives behind war are lethally dangerous, because an entire group of industries rely on war to stay in business. Therefore, **they are incentivized to politically antagonize and encourage war as a necessity to fulfill their business goals**. Incentivizing war is obviously contrary to the benefit of society; encouraging division and otherness through media to turn groups against each other by creating enemy images. Artificially created division between groups is a well-documented commonly employed tactic throughout history.

My personal experience with this involves traveling in the summer of 2003 to the predominantly Muslim country of Turkey. While I was there I wore the same surfer/skater American clothes I was wearing in Hawaii. I had my skateboard with me (I had been skating around Europe), and I stood out like a sore thumb. When I visited mosques, and during prayer times, it was obvious that I was not a Muslim, and likely American or European. However, I found the Muslim people of Turkey to be some of the kindest and sweetest people in all my travels. Similarly, I have Muslim friends from Egypt that I lived and worked with in L.A., also very generous, sweet, helpful people. I have Palestinian Muslim friends that live in the bay area, and they are one of the sweetest most loving families I know. When I told the mother in the family that my Dad was Jewish, she said, "Awwww we love Jewish people."

My encounters with Muslim people have been wonderful to say the least. And yet I am often told by some of the mainstream media that Muslims are all extremists who want to kill me and my family for not being Muslim, and this is somehow part of their religion. So why haven't any of my Muslim friends questioned my religious and spiritual faith? Why have they been so good to me knowing that I'm American with a very Jewish last name? The easy answer to these questions is that blanket extremist claims about Islam are not true. Islam is just like Christianity or any other religion in the respect that a small portion of people choose to be extreme about it or are turned extremist by war and poverty. However, most Muslims (all the ones I've met) are normal loving good people that don't take their religion too seriously.

Having a positive experience in a Muslim country has given me the frame of reference to critically think the mainstream media's agenda artificially encouraging a fear of Islam; and it deeply saddens me to see these claims being made about Muslims. However, if I were a conspiracy theorist, I would hypothesize that these are divisive tactics employed by the military industrial complex, to create an enemy image of Muslims, making false claims about the majority of Islam, ensuring that Americans will approve of war and military occupation in the middle east. Either way, this type of divisiveness is counterproductive to cooperation and world peace, while devastating communities in the middle east.

Furthermore, U.S. presidents have unilaterally supported Saudi Arabia, the most Muslim extremist country in the region, while bombing and destroying the most moderate Muslim countries like Iraq and Syria. The Saudi's have given us Wahhabism, Al Queda, ISIS, the Bin Laden family, and the 9-11 hijackers. Yet Saudi Arabia has financial and military support from the U.S. government and every sitting president. However, **countries like Iraq and Syria were previously moderate muslim places where many Christians**

lived without the threat of extremism, and yet American invasion encouraged the rise of Muslim extremists.

Afghanistan was once a beautiful, moderate, and prosperous country before it was invaded by the Soviet Union. The U.S. financially and militarily supported Muslim extremists, the Mujahideen, to fight the Soviets. After winning, the Mujahideen became known as the Taliban. And the Taliban was originally supported by the U.S. as a legitimate government, until they were accused of involvement in 9-11.

There is an odd pattern of the U.S. government supporting and encouraging violent Muslim extremism, while eliminating moderate non-violent Muslims. U.S. Congresswomen and Iraq War veteran Tulsi Gabbard has spoken out on this issue, and described a similar pattern caused by U.S. military regime change policy in the middle east.

Meanwhile, mainstream media has "analysts" and "experts" portray to the public that all Muslims are extremists. It seems like the perfect divisive tactic to sell weapons and profit from war. How do we abandon this artificially created tragic division of cultures? How do we create cooperation and peace on this planet?

Pursuing an answer to these questions brings us back to Erich Fromm and his book, *To Have or To Be?* Fromm argues that *having* and *being* are two oppositional modes of existence. In the having mode of existence, a person connects to what he can possess and control, which inevitably leads to violence and domination. In the being mode of existence, a person appreciates the magic and beauty of creation, humanity, and society without possession or control, but rather adding to and assisting the natural growth process of life.

Fromm eloquently describes the being mode of existence in the following way:

> *The mode of being has as its prerequisites independence,*
> *freedom, and the presence of critical reason. Its*
> *fundamental characteristic is that of being active... To*
> *be active means to give expression to one's faculties,*
> *talents, to the wealth of human gifts with which- though*
> *in varying degrees- every human being is endowed.*
> *It means to renew oneself, to grow, to flow out, to*
> *love, to transcend the prison of one's isolated ego...*

In an article written by Fromm, published in *The Saturday Review* in 1964, he poetically describes the *necrophilous* character of the having mode of existence:

> *While life is characterized by growth in a structured,*
> *functional manner, the necrophilous person loves all that*
> *does not grow, all that is mechanical. The necrophilous*
> *person is driven by the desire to transform the organic*
> *into the inorganic, to approach life mechanically, as if*
> *all living persons were things... Memory, rather than*
> *experience; having, rather than being, is what counts.*
> *The necrophilous person can relate to an object- a*
> *flower or a person- only if he possesses it; hence a*
> *threat to his possession is a threat to himself; if he loses*
> *possession he loses contact with the world... He loves*
> *control, and in the act of controlling he kills life.*

If Fromm's assessment is correct, the having mode of existence is responsible for the systemic spreading of violent competitive hier- archical dominance; while learning more about the being mode of existence would benefit peace and cooperation. Engaging the being mode of existence is a brave challenge in a system built on a foundation of possession. However, Fromm believed that the having mode of existence would burn people out, causing catastrophic psychological, economic, and sociological disasters. Perhaps we are seeing those disasters now, as many aspects of society seem to be falling apart. Therefore, how do we create a social structure that encourages the being mode of existence?

The foundational thought on being in sustainable peaceful unification involves encouraging individual talents and passions within a structure of cooperation and simplicity. Indigenous cultures often employed a simplistic view of ownership- they didn't believe in it. Therefore, land and resources were shared, housing was built based upon need, and people worked together to procure food, clothing, and tools. These systems worked for thousands of years, and often peacefully. The problem with applying this idea to the modern context is that we are already so deep in private property, advanced technology, and a hierarchy of dominance, that it is hard for many people to imagine voluntarily living so simply and happily. In the Chinese and Soviet totalitarian communist version of government, when these values were forced upon people it ran contrary to the philosophy of cooperation and non-violence.

However, in the blending of ideas, and in applying a "this and that" philosophy, perhaps a third thought emerges; creating a baseline of needs-met opportunities for cooperation minded people to co-exist with free market capitalism, and a tinge of reasonable socialism. For example, if large amounts of public property are designated to create food forests, then would-be homeless, disenfranchised, or even relaxed people could camp and obtain food from the forest. They can choose to live somewhat like indigenous subsistence cultures did for thousands of years. In this example no-one is being forced to live that way, but the opportunity is there. At least people who feel they don't fit into the workforce, or for whatever reason could not continue to work a job, would have somewhere to go.

In this cooperative model, police, military, legislation, courts, and prisons only exist to keep people from hurting one another. Murder, violence, sexual assault, theft, and fraud are the only reasons to imprison or rehabilitate a member of society. Prisons should be a very comfortable healing place that give non-violent communication sessions, therapy, exercise, gardening, and counseling to inmates so that they can come out into society healed and ready to share their gifts in a positive helpful way. People learn violent and abusive strategies, usually because they have been subjected to violence and abuse. Therefore, these people need healing, not more pain and punishment.

However, to truly heal our sick social systems and create a tranquil sustainable future for all of humanity, **we must eliminate the underlying mechanisms that cause conflicts of interest**. It is deeply unfortunate that our current economic and monetary systems incentivize people, who might otherwise do good, to buy into the emperors new clothing and perpetuate fraud. Additionally there is punishment for whistleblowers, non-participants, revolutionaries, and freedom seekers.

Many politicians rely on corporate money to fund their campaigns. Television and newsprint media require advertising for funding, and therefore cannot write stories against the interest of their corporate advertisers. Mining companies need to destroy ecosystems to obtain raw materials for profit. Pharmaceutical companies make more money when people are dependent on drugs. The private prison industry needs strict drug laws to obtain prisoners; to turn a profit. Weapons manufacturers need war to stay in business. Narrative based teachers need obedient student-like receptacles to deposit information and fulfill department of education requirements. The military industrial complex needs a percentage of the population to have limited opportunities to incentivize and encourage military enrollment. All of these examples of an underlying cause: conflicts of interest.

Examples of conflicts of interest are everywhere around us. If I'm honest with myself, I participate in conflicts of interest every time I drive a car, pay taxes, use electricity, buy a consumer product, or hoard wealth. My perspective and assessment of the systemic root cause of conflicts of interest involves unhealthy competition for money, power, and economic inflation driving an increased desperation to just meet basic needs. In other words, the general population is increasingly working more for less money and abundance, while the global elite have mechanisms to maintain political power, economic design, wealth, and dominance.

It is a most unfortunate defect of our current monetary system that conflicts of interest poison and defile aspects of society that rely on purity. Examples of conflicts of interest include:

- Politicians need corporate campaign contributions so they can finance a competitive campaign, and obtain mainstream media worthy status. Therefore their policy choices reflect the needs of their financiers, rather than representing their voting constituents.

- Media relies on corporate advertising to stay in business. Therefore they cannot report a story that is antithetical to the interests of their corporate sponsors, for fear of losing advertising. Media thus becomes lock and key with the political agenda of its corporate sponsors.

- The pastor, minister, or reverend that needs church membership money to upkeep the facility and pay himself for his basic needs and the needs of his family. Therefore, they find themselves in the awkward position of marketing and selling spirituality.

- Individuals who choose romantic relationships for financial stability, and choose to stay with a "breadwinner" regardless of disconnect or abuse in the relationship, because the underlying need for financial security creates a strong fear of lack.

- People who choose jobs and careers for financial security; such as joining the military, or simply working a job that isn't reflective of their individual talents, gifts and excitement. They become antithetical to their own sense of self, health and wellness just to meet basic financial needs in an economic system that requires a percentage of the population to make that choice. In this model it can become someones job to bomb another country, kill other people, poison families, or destroy a place; which is contrary to people's sense of love, purpose, and spirituality. Hence the trauma and PTSD that is rampant as a result of military service, mining, chemical production sites, etc.

I don't specifically know how we can transform this insane mess of a global economic system that we currently find ourselves in, and I haven't developed a proposal for an alternative system. However, what I do know is that it starts with meeting peoples basic needs. Food, shelter, clothing, safety, and dignity is a universal human birthright. **All people deserve the opportunity to cultivate land, build a home, and live a natural life free from the monopoly game competition for private property dog eat dog mentality**.

Through cooperation we may find our way out of these situations and circumstances. We may find that we feel better when our society is at peace; enjoying a government that is free from conflicts of interest, and truly acting out of what's best for the population; when our prisons are strictly for rehabilitating violent threats; and when the homeless or disenfranchised have access to therapy and a food forest with camp ground facilities.

Creating a cooperative environment that nurtures the being mode of existence is crucial for the development and practice of individual synchronicity, mysticism, and the natural spiritual path. Our society can be built and structured in such a way that it is conducive to the depth of synchronicity, by meeting peoples baseline needs first: shelter, food, water, family, community, activity, health, safety, freedom, and love. When those baseline needs are met, then perhaps a more advanced stage of social values will precipitate.

Human desire for innovation and technology can develop healthfully when we base our economy and value on the true gifts and talents of the individual, who will naturally work cooperatively because his needs for a positive family and community have been met. To obtain that sort of world, we must find the spiritual alignment within ourselves and communicate and teach that alignment to our children. When we collectively come into alignment with spirit, humanity, and earth, we will have heaven on earth.

The Te-Tao Ching, Chapter 78, Robert Henricks translation leaves us with this insight:

> *In the whole world, nothing is softer*
> *and weaker than water.*
>
> *And yet for attacking the hard and strong, nothing can*
> *beat it, because there is nothing you can use to replace it.*
>
> *The water can defeat the unyielding-*
>
> *That the weak can defeat the strong-*
>
> *There is no-one in the world who doesn't know it, and*
> *yet there is no-one who can put it into practice.*
>
> *For this reason, the words of the Sage say:*
>
> *To take on yourself the disgrace of the state- this is*
> *called being the lord of altars of earth and grain;*
>
> *To assume responsibility for ill-omened events in*
> *the state- this is called being king of the world.*
>
> *Correct words seem to say the reverse*
> *of what you expect them to say.*

ALIGNMENT

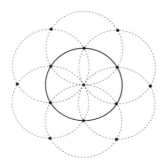

And when he (Jesus) was demanded of the Pharisees, when the
kingdom of God should come, he answered them and said, "The
kingdom of God cometh not with observation: Neither shall they say,
Lo here! or, lo there! for, behold, the kingdom of God is within you.

-Luke 17:20 KJV

WHEN I DISCOVERED my tingling sensational synchronicity, I was in a very aligned state. I found that in denying myself
of worldly habitual distractions, I was able to tap into profound
aspects of my being. I would later discover that I could easily slip
back into my old habitual negative programming if I wasn't careful.
I found that spiritual alignment is something that can teeter totter
depending on the beliefs we choose to buy into, and the diligence of

mining the subconscious for the intent purpose of redefining negative beliefs, and bringing our definitions into alignment with love, peace, and excitement.

I have heard it said, "If it isn't based in love, it isn't true." I'm not sure where that quote comes from, but it resonates with my personal experience.

Aligning with love, joy, peace, and excitement, is the path that brings the greatest health and healing. However, we cannot simply glaze over our negative belief patterns and pretend like they don't exist. In doing so, we are prone to manifest events that will trigger those negative beliefs and subsequent emotions. **We must first be honest with ourselves about who we are and what kind of negative beliefs we have bought into**, so that we can drop the baggage that doesn't belong to us.

When I became a spiritually minded person, I made the mistake of suppressing my negative patterns, beliefs, and definitions. I was so enthralled with following the magic of synchronicity, that I assumed I was beyond previous negative experiences. This was a huge mistake on my part and would come back to bite me hard.

When a distasteful experience triggered a negative emotional response, my defense mechanisms would justify the response. I would remind myself of my magical spiritual synchronicity, and I would tell myself a corresponding story that painted me in the right and them in the wrong. I wasn't taking the time to mine my negative subconscious belief systems and remove the baggage that didn't belong to me. This led to more manifestations of negative synchronicity until I was deeply embedded in some very painful circumstances. At times I habitually chose to double down on my negative responses, going even deeper into the pain and suffering.

I repeated some of the same patterns before I realized that they were coming from my subconscious programming. I started to realize that I had negative strategies for love, connection, and empathy, and that I needed to learn how to love and heal myself. Around this time, I badly injured my back, and was forced to lie in bed for weeks. **The back injury turned out to be the medicine I needed**, and I meditated for hours each day on healing my childhood trauma and negative subconscious belief system programming. I successfully found the most injured parts of myself and redefined the fear that was keeping me out of alignment.

During this process, one of the clearest communications I received from spirit, is that my manifestation of abundance is connected to writing and sharing my stories. Essentially my gift to share with world is that I'm a storyteller, and my unique story to share involves *the depth of synchronicity*. Therefore, writing this book has been about coming into a greater depth of alignment for me. As I've gotten deeper into telling this story and sharing my ideas, my health, peace, excitement, and love levels have significantly increased. I'm finally getting this story off my chest, and in this process my abundance has already manifested in ways beyond what I could have imagined.

Sharing my synchronicity, alignment, values, ideas, adventure, and spiritual phenomena stories with all of you readers has been very healing for me, representing my highest excitement. Paradoxically, when I'm following my highest excitement I feel calm, peaceful, and tranquil. The energy of excitement and joy is the indication of spiritual alignment.

Communicating my spiritual alignment and healing process is like casting a spell. When you spell something out, words become power and magic.

"In the beginning was the Word, and the Word was with God, and the Word was God."

-John 1:1 KJV

Words are sound; sound is vibration; vibrations are waves; according to quantum physics, when we aren't looking at particles, they exist as waves. Vibrational waves are the foundation for all that exists. Therefore, if John was correct, then **God is the subtle vibrational wave function of All That Is.**

Words are magic creators, and yet silence is perhaps even more powerful. One of the most effective activities I've discovered to increase my alignment, awareness, and inner peace, has been fasting from words. After many full days of silent meditations and no hearing or reading of words, I experienced the reduction of my egoic personality feedback loop, which ordinarily reinforces itself by speaking. Words can be positive and powerful, but silence can be even more powerful.

The Buddha achieved alignment or enlightenment after many consecutive days of silent meditation under the Bodhi tree. Jesus fasted for forty days in the Judaean desert. Many Native American and Aboriginal cultures practice a spirit quest that involved days of silence, fasting, and time in nature. These quests for alignment and enlightenment have common threads: silence, nature, and fasting; interrupting and quieting the habitual egoic structure.

Chapter 48 of the Te-Tao Ching tells us:

Those who work at their studies increase day after day.

Those who have heard the Tao decrease day after day.

They decrease and decrease, till they get
to the point where they do nothing.

They do nothing and yet there's nothing left undone.

This verse describes the great spiritual masters that have been found meditating for days, or even weeks. They get to a point where they are almost literally doing nothing. However, what they are doing is raising their vibration, frequency, and energy, and perhaps astral traveling in various realms and dimensions. Through the purification of consciousness, manifestations of earth can shift from one version of earth to another. The greater the alignment, the greater shift in vibrational frequency, the more different the version of earth that can be manifested.

The E.T channel known as Bashar once exclaimed, "The greatest power requires the lightest touch. When you truly know you have power, you don't have to do anything at all to make things happen. You simply allow creation to work perfectly, because it already is."

Those who use spirituality and religion to try to force others, or manipulate people, are playing the part of violent extremists; pushing away the natural energy of unconditional love that is God. Religious extremism involves the idea that one religion, belief, or practice is superior to another. It espouses that others are wrong, and they will be punished in one way or another for their spiritual beliefs. Unfortunately, we see this idea commonly communicated in the major religions. Christian extremists believe that God will send people to hell if they don't get baptized or accept Jesus as their lord and savior. Muslim extremists have their version of violence and persecution on many levels. Zionist Jews believe that they are God's chosen people, and that they must remove all the Muslims from the "holy land". These patriarchal biblical religions offer forms of extremism that involve their beliefs being right, while other spiritual beliefs are characterized as wrong.

This is a very dangerous belief, because it is the foundational belief that generates and branches out into prejudice, domination, and cultural genocide. Historically and paradoxically the Christian religions have taken most of the world through extremist violence. The Spanish inquisition, the crusades, and European imperialism around the world were done in the name of God and Christ. However, these acts were quite contradictory to the teachings of Christ that we should love our enemies and pray for those who harm us.

Personally, I don't believe it was Christ intention to create a religion or church. He spoke out against institutions and governments. He was a free-thinking radical of his time that preached the individual's connection to God. When asked by the Pharisees when the kingdom of God was coming, Jesus said, "...behold, the kingdom of God is within you." He then gave teachings, instructions, and examples of how to find our personal alignment with the kingdom of God that is already present in each of us.

Alignment and clarity about the path of alignment can be achieved through drastic shifts, such as the path taken by the Buddha or Christ. However, alignment is also a process that can be taken in baby steps. I have found that my path of alignment has been a combination of both drastic shifts, such as fasting and days of silence in nature, or simply meditating daily and making little changes in my life. It can be taken on a case by case basis, depending on the need of the individual.

In his book Man and His Symbols, Carl Jung wrote:

The individual is the only reality. The further we move away from the individual toward abstract ideas about Homo sapiens, the more likely we are to fall into error.

Jung was writing in the context of dream analysis and clinical psychology. And he was specifically sharing an example of his relationship with Sigmund Freud, describing the contrast between their philosophical differences and how it affected their relationship. Jung uses this example to make the point that mechanical techniques and generalized values of interpretation cannot be applied to individual psychic personalities. In other words, we cannot merely apply a one size fits all diagnosis or viewpoint to the complexity of an individual.

Jung shares an example of Freud's interpretation of one of Jung's dreams, in which he lied to Freud to remain in agreement with the interpretation, because he knew Freud well enough to know that he didn't want to disagree with his technique and sacrifice his relationship with him. Jung confesses that he felt bad about lying, but he was afraid that if he shared his personal dream interpretation and his inner world with Freud, he might risk sacrificing their friendship.

In this fascinating story between two of the founding fathers of modern psychology, Jung goes on to describe that while searching for answers he thought Freud would find suitable, he had an intuitive realization that was so powerful it changed his psychological understanding and caused him to depart from Freud's interpretations. Jung's insight was that, "my dream meant *myself*, *my* life and *my* world, my whole reality against a theoretical structure erected by another, strange mind for reasons and purposes of its own. It was not Freud's dream, it was mine; and I understood suddenly in a flash what my dream meant."

I believe whole-heartedly in the individual's right to interpret his or her life in the way that works for them. When we understand ourselves more fully and completely, we can disassociate from the baggage and expectations of others, and step into the alignment of individual health and healing that is the true vibration of every soul powered human on the planet, and perhaps every being in the universe.

Alignment is our greatest gift, because it gives us health, peace, abundance, comfort, love, and excitement. When Jesus responded to the Pharisees saying, "The Kingdom of God is within you," I believe he meant that we always have direct access to god as a spiritual birthright, regardless of an institution's agenda to interpret god for us; that we can access and find our own version of personal alignment with spirit. When we remove the inherited negative beliefs and actions that don't belong to us, we allow ourselves to align with the energy of God that is already within us.

This is the process of spiritual alchemy. The transformation of disease to health, negative to positive, dark to light, is a process of coming into alignment with who and what we already are. It is simply the choice to stop blocking and holding ourselves down with negative beliefs and actions. The beautiful simplicity of purification is that it involves allowing the true self to shine and letting go of all that doesn't belong to us. Love is positive energy characterized by that which binds, unifies, and makes things whole. Contrasting that, negative energy is that which separates, segregates, and breaks apart. God is the energy of love, the binding force of creation.

Bringing it full circle to the profound life changing verse I was contemplating in 2004, from Robert Henricks translation of the Tao, chapter 1:

As for the Way, the Way that can be
spoken of is not the constant Way;

As for names, the name that can be
named is not the constant name.

The nameless is the beginning of the ten thousand
things (the earth and all its features).

The named is the mother of the ten thousand things.

Therefore, those constantly without desires,
by this means will perceive its subtlety.

Those constantly with desires, by this means will
see only that which they yearn for and seek.

These two together emerge;

They have different names yet they're called the same;

That which is even more profound than the profound-

The gateway of all subtleties.

This mysterious riddle of a verse speaks to the profound impact that desire has on spiritual alignment. What I found confusing at first, was the idea of being *constantly without desires.*

The depth of desire permeates all of physical reality; even desiring not to desire is still a form of desire. What I eventually realized is that the desire to be in alignment with what I need for growth and optimum health is crucially important to identify and cultivate. Therefore, **desire can be categorized as healthy or unhealthy depending on what it aims to acquire.**

The universe will not always give us what we want, but we always get what we need to grow and evolve. Spiritual manifestation is not about getting whatever one wants, but rather aligning oneself with what one needs. If my desires are in alignment with what I need for optimum health, growth, and evolution, then I am in alignment with the spiritual power to manifest my reality without resistance.

Lao Tzu, the mythical author of the Tao, describes being constantly without desire as a means to perceive the subtlety of the way of heaven. Conversely, he describes being *constantly with desire* as trap that leads to seeing only that which one *yearns for and seeks*; like tunnel vision. However, he then combines these contrasting modes of desire with, *these two together emerge...the gateway of all subtleties*. This is the great depth of spiritual alchemy, the crucial point of finding balance or power in combining opposing forces. I interpret this to mean that **when human desire is merged with the way of heaven; the path of the soul; when ones desires are aligned with what one needs for optimum health, growth and evolution; that individual will access true spiritual alignment resulting in truly powerful manifestations.**

For example, I may want to buy an off-grid farm house property, install solar panels, and create a food forest for self sufficiency. However, I may need to go through a process to get to that point, or I may need to learn other lessons and have other experiences relevant to my growth and health as a soul having a human experience; in which case the entire off-grid farm dream may not be in my soul's realm of manifestation. However wonderful and earth friendly it may sound, it won't happen for me unless I need to experience that life relevant to my personal growth process.

Therefore clarity and perception about what is relevant and genuinely exciting to pursue is crucial in discovering ones individual alignment. Mediation, energy identification, and the awareness of synchronicity are important tools to help us discover our soul's path. The feeling of excitement translates as the energetic indication of what the soul or higher mind has planned, and like a thread it leads to all other forms of excitement, if one is willing to let go of ego expectations.

Alchemically merging the idea of free will with fate and finding the perfect balance between the two; the analogy of going down the hallway of destiny in a way that one chooses: walking, running, jumping, dancing, etc; these are ideas to explore in the depth of synchronicity and the path of spiritual alignment.

Synchronicity is the guiding force, the reflective communication from spirit, that displays and indicates the quality of each one's individual vibrational alignment. Alignment is our true essence and our birthright. We are all deserving of alignment with love and light. All beings are made of love, and all beings are blessed.

POST SCRIPT-
SYNCHRONICITY
WITH C.G. JUNG

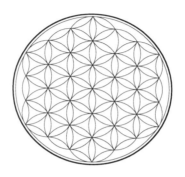

IN THE SPRING of 2018 I suddenly became interested in research-ing alchemy. I read a few books, learned about Hermes Thoth, the Philosophers Stone, and other basic historical themes of alchemy. Then in the summer of 2018 I made the decision to get serious about writing my vulnerable personal story on *The Depth of Synchronicity*. However, I was not expecting that my research into the academic and historical context surrounding the word synchronicity would connect with my new-found interest in alchemy.

To properly write about my experience with synchronicity, I needed to research the man who coined the term and brought it into the academic world. As I read through some of Jung's work on the synchronicity, I was surprised to find that C.G Jung devoted much of his academic work to the subject of alchemy. A close friend and colleague of Jung, Marie-Louise von Franz, in her book *Alchemy, An Introduction to the Symbolism and the Psychology*, writes that Jung "devoted many years of study to this subject (alchemy), which he practically dug up from the dunghill of the past, for it was a forgotten and despised field of investigation which he has suddenly revived."

Dr. von Franz goes on in her introduction to explain that Jung had become interested in alchemy because of a synchronous experience. Apparently one of his patients was sharing a dream in which she (the patient) had dreamt of an eagle that was eating its own wings. Intuitively Dr. Jung felt that this motif was an archetypal product of the collective unconscious with historical parallels, yet he had no context or clue as to where it could be found in any literature. However, Jung would soon discover *The Ripley Scroll*, which shares pictures of the alchemical process. As he examined this obscure text on alchemy, he was surprised to find his patient's dream motif: a picture of the eagle eating its own wings. This synchronicity sparked Jung's initial interest in alchemy, which would eventually lead to him becoming one of the most prolific scholarly authorities on the subject; tying alchemy into his practice and teaching of psychological dream analysis.

I felt it an exciting and peculiar synchronicity that I had just suddenly began to research alchemy, while simultaneously researching Jung for his work on synchronicity, only to discover that Jung devoted a huge portion of his life's work to alchemy as well. Additionally, to discover that Jung was inspired to study alchemy because of a synchronous event, was an exciting discovery. However, this was just the beginning of my synchronicity with Jung's works.

As I read Jung's book **Synchronicity, An Acausal Connecting Principe**, I learned that he compares the idea of synchronicity to

Richard Wilhelm's translation of the concept of the Tao. My own personal and unique story, essentially the story of my life, has been greatly influenced by the Tao Te Ching. The reader will notice multiple references to the ancient Chinese philosophy in the pages of this book. It would have been impossible for me to write my story without mentioning the Tao, as it is so intrinsically connected to my personal story. I find it fascinating that upon researching Jung's work into synchronicity, as I prepare to tell my own story about what I call *the depth of synchronicity,* I discover that Jung also connects the idea of synchronicity with the Tao Te Ching.

Furthermore, in the introductory foreword of Jung's book on synchronicity, Sonu Shamdasani writes that in 1928 Jung received a copy of the "Taoist alchemical treatise *The Secret of the Golden Flower*" from the translator Richard Wilhelm, asking Jung to write a commentary. Receiving the "Taoist alchemical treatise" caused Jung to "set aside his work" and "not publish it." It seems he was dramatically influenced to change course and, "Instead he devoted himself to the cross-cultural study of the individuation process, focusing on medieval alchemy in particular". Again, I was excited to see Taoism and Alchemy referenced in the introduction to Jung's book on synchronicity.

Although these are relatively minor synchronicities compared to some of the experiences in my story, it has been a fun set of "meaningful coincidences" to observe how my academic and philosophical interests have coincided with Jung's.

BIBLIOGRAPHY

Henricks, Robert. *Lao-Tzu Te-Tao Ching.* New York: Ballantine Books, 1989. Print.

Fromm, Erich. *To Have Or To Be?.* New York: Bloomsbury Academic, 2013. Print.

Cooper, Bill. *Behold a Pale Horse.* Arizona: Light Technology Publications, 1991. Print.

Jung, C.G.. *Synchronicity.* New Jersey: Princeton University Press, 1973. Print.

Hauck, Dennis William. *The Emerald Tablet, Alchemy For Personal Transformation.* England: Penguin Compass, 1999. Print

Holymard, E.J.. *Alchemy.* England: Penguin Books, 1968. Print.

Franz, Marie-Louise von. *Alchemy, An Introduction to the Symbolism and the Psychology.* Canada: Inner City Books, 1980. Print.

Jung, C.G.. *Aion.* New York: Routledge, 1981. Print.

Jung, C.G. and Pauli, Wolfgang. *Atom and Archetype.* New Jersey: Princeton University Press, 2001. Print.

Talbot, Michael. *The Holographic Universe.* New York: Harper Perennial, 1992. Print.

Bohm, David. *Wholeness and the Implicate Order.* New York: Routledge, 2006. Print.

Jung, C.G.. *Man and his Symbols.* U.S.A: Dell Publishing, 1968. Print.

Smith, Dr. Jane Ma'ati. *The Emerald Tablet of Hermes and The Kybalion.* California: Dr. Jane Ma'ati Smith, 2008. Print.

Castaneda, Carlos. *The Fire From Within.* New York: Washington Square Press, 1991. Print.

Lipton, Dr. Bruce. *The Biology of Belief.* California: Mountain of Love/Elite Books, 2005. Print.

Brogan, Dr. Kelly. *A Mind of Your Own.* New York: HarperCollins Publishers, 2016. Print.

Thomas, Kelan; Malcolm, Benjamin; Lastra, Dan. *Psilocybin-Assisted Therapy: A Review of a Novel Treatment for Psychiatric Disorders.* Volume 49, Issue 5: Journal of Psychoactive Drugs, November-December 2017. Internet.

Carhart-Harris, Robin L. *The Therapeutic Potential of Psychedelic Drugs: Past, Present, and Future.* Neuropsychopharmacology volume 42, April 26, 2017. Internet.

Sessa, Dr. Ben and Worthley, Eileen. *Psychedelic Drug Treatments.* Virginia: Mercury Learning and Information, 2016. Print.

Castaneda, Carlos. *The Art Of Dreaming.* New York: HarperCollins Publishers, 1993. Print.

Freire, Paulo. *Pedagogy of the Oppressed.* New York: Continuum International, 2000. Print.

Rosenberg, Dr. Marshall. *Nonviolent Communication, A Language of Life.* California: PuddleDancer Press, 2015. Print.

Marx, Karl. *Das Kapital.* United States: Pacific Publishing Studio, 2010. Print.

Ereira, Allan. *The Heart of the World.* London: Jonathan Cape, 1990. Print.

Zinn, Howard. *A Peoples History of the United States.* New York: Harper Perennial, 2005. Print.

Sai, Dr. David Keanu. *Ua Mau Ke Ea, Sovereignty Endures: An Overview of the Political and Legal History of the Hawaiian Islands.* Hawaii: Pu'a Foundation, 2011. Print.

Kane, Herb. *Voyagers.* Washington: WhaleSong, 1991. Print.

Kane, Herb. *Ancient Hawaii.* Hawaii: The Kawainui Press, 1997. Print